Mental Canvas for Training and Development

Creating Engaging, Interactive Presentations

Michael Commini

apress®

Mental Canvas for Training and Development: Creating Engaging, Interactive Presentations

Michael Commini
Santa Fe, NM, USA

ISBN-13 (pbk): 978-1-4842-8773-6   ISBN-13 (electronic): 978-1-4842-8774-3
https://doi.org/10.1007/978-1-4842-8774-3

Managing Director, Apress Media LLC: Welmoed Spahr
Acquisitions Editor: Miriam Haidara
Development Editor: James Markham
Project Manager: Jessica Vakili

Distributed to the book trade worldwide by Springer Science+Business Media New York, 1 NY Plaza, New York, NY 10004. Phone 1-800-SPRINGER, fax (201) 348-4505, e-mail orders-ny@springer-sbm.com, or visit www.springeronline.com. Apress Media, LLC is a California LLC and the sole member (owner) is Springer Science + Business Media Finance Inc (SSBM Finance Inc). SSBM Finance Inc is a **Delaware** corporation.

For information on translations, please e-mail booktranslations@springernature.com; for reprint, paperback, or audio rights, please e-mail bookpermissions@springernature.com.

Apress titles may be purchased in bulk for academic, corporate, or promotional use. eBook versions and licenses are also available for most titles. For more information, reference our Print and eBook Bulk Sales web page at http://www.apress.com/bulk-sales.

Any source code or other supplementary material referenced by the author in this book is available to readers on the Github repository: https://github.com/Apress/Mental-Canvas-for-Training-and-Development. For more detailed information, please visit https://www.apress.com/gp/services/source-code.

Paper in this product is recyclable.

This work is dedicated to the training and development professionals at Saudi Aramco. The eight years I spent working with each of you gave me new perspectives from which to engage those adult learners with whom I was privileged to share my knowledge and experience.

Table of Contents

About the Author

Dr. Michael Commini recently retired from Saudi Aramco, the world's largest oil company, where he designed, developed, and delivered workshops for competency-based career succession as well as competency-based development maps. He built and refined his experience in training and development while serving in the US Air Force. After leaving the Air Force, he co-founded TechNET Software TeKnowledgies® (TST), an educational software development company. Among TST's clients were the Texas Naval JrROTC, the Saenger Organization, UPS®, and Lanier Worldwide®. In addition to his work with TST, Dr. Commini served in the 1990s as a college professor teaching electronics, mathematics, computer networking, and data communications for ITT Technical Institute. He was also privileged to have worked at the US Joint Forces Command, Joint Warfighting Center, Joint Knowledge Development and Distribution Capability, where he was the lead knowledge management analyst and project manager for one of the world's largest and most diverse instructional design teams prior to moving to Saudi Arabia. He now resides in the Dominican Republic with his dog, Diamond, where he meets people from all walks of life and smokes good cigars.

Acknowledgments

I would like to acknowledge the following people at Saudi Aramco:

- Muhammed Ovais – My peer and co-worker. Together we were privileged to guide many senior staff through the development of competency-based training and development maps. You kept me sane and became one of my closest friends in Saudi Arabia.

- Rheman Aktar – I cried with you when your first wife passed, and I celebrated with you when you were blessed by God with a new wife. Your positive outlook on life even in the face of extreme hardships was a blessing to those of us privileged to call you teammate. We enjoyed good food and great companionship. I miss that.

- Dr. Edward Shelton – Your books and ideas on transformational leadership and your mentorship of each of your teammates were truly inspirational. It was a privilege to have you on my dissertation committee.

- Tony Arden – Perhaps one of the best division heads I have ever met and worked for. Not only did you counteract the transactional leaders' poor decisions, you took them under your wing and actually helped them change from poorly respected transactional leaders to transformational leaders others would follow.

ACKNOWLEDGMENTS

- Rheem Ghanim – You were the model by which I
  measured all other division heads for whom I worked.
  You were the reason I was privileged to work for Saudi
  Aramco, and you taught me what true transformational
  leadership is. Thank you.

I would also like to acknowledge the following people at PetroSkills:

- J. Ford Brett – Your vision and leadership inspired
  me to learn and understand what competency-based
  development is.

- Ron Hinn – Together with Ford, you gave this old goat
  the chance to share his knowledge and ideas with
  leaders from all over the world.

And I would like to acknowledge the many professors in the
instructional design program at Capella University. Special recognition
should go to Dr. Jim McDermott, my dissertation committee chair. You
motivated me to keep writing even as I suffered the loss of both my
parents. Your mentorship will be remembered fondly for the rest of my life.

And finally, to Dr. Julie Dorsey and the team of researchers at Yale
University. You envisioned a world in which 2D digital art could come alive
in a 3D world. Without you, Mental Canvas would not exist!

Introduction

Since the beginning of time, mankind has used various methods to communicate ideas and share knowledge. Hand signals, smoke signals, flags, light, drawings – all technologies easily available to man down through the ages. As we entered into the late 19th and early 20th centuries, telegraph and telephone were added – for the first time using the medium of electricity to remain in contact with those we loved and to communicate with our peers!

As the 20th century progressed, so too did the technologies available to us. Marconi invented the radio and Farnsworth the electronic television. Both were used by the military to communicate across vast distances. And both were used by educators to deliver instructional content to listeners and viewers with varying degrees of success. For example, most Americans are very familiar with the *Public Broadcasting Service* (PBS) and the educational offerings available to children – *Sesame Street, The Electric Company, Reading Rainbow, and Sid the Science Kid,* just to name a few. As technologies continued to advance, academics sought new ways to adapt that technology for the educational benefit of children, teens, and adults.

And, of course, we never stopped learning about learning. We never stopped investigating ways in which people transfer knowledge from one individual to another. It is beyond the scope of this book to debate whether people have learning "styles" or learning "preferences." And the theories of learning are many – from Pavlov and his theory of behavioral conditioning to Piaget and his theory of cognitive development, to Vygotsky and his theory of social development, new observations and theories of how we learn appear every time a new psychologist wants to make a name for herself.

One thing is clear. Whether you believe you are a visual learner, an auditory learner, a kinesthetic learner, a logical learner, or some combination of the currently propounded styles of learning, each "style" can be used to enhance each other "style" and thus help in knowledge transfer. That includes the visual arts.

Think back to when you were a child listening to your dad as he read you a bedtime story. Did that book have pictures used to enhance your understanding of the material? Did the fairy-tale book your mother read to you include pictures of fairies, castles, and damsels in distress? Those images helped to enhance your understanding of what fairies, castles, and damsels in distress are and how they look.

Later, as you entered school and began learning the material some adult somewhere decided you needed to learn, did your textbooks include pictures and illustrations? Did those pictures and illustrations visually explain the information the textbook author was presenting? The answer, of course, is "yes." If the author and publisher did their jobs properly, every image and illustration used within the book was designed to enhance your understanding of the material.

That is because we human beings are visual creatures. We depend on our eyes to convey information to our brains that we then use to improve our lives. Our very survival sometimes depends on our sense of sight. Do you doubt the veracity of that statement? Go to a busy intersection in your city or town and stand on the corner. Close your eyes and listen to the traffic as it swishes past the corner. With your eyes closed, can you tell when it is safe to cross the street?

That exercise is near and dear to my heart as it is the same exercise my father, blinded in *World War II*, taught me at a young age when conveying the importance of paying attention to one's surroundings. A lesson especially necessary if one is to guide a person who is without sight. My father used his knowledge of sight, and its visual cues, to transfer the knowledge of (1) using landmarks to find one's way between destinations, (2) when it is safe to cross a busy street, (3) how to guide a blind person around, over or under obstacles with minimal safety risks, (4) count money, and (5) appreciate art and how artists use their work to convey ideas.

You see, my father was a budding artist of some small renown in his hometown before he was drafted and inducted into the army. And like artists everywhere, he used his drawings to convey emotions, ideas, and concepts that touched peoples' hearts and moved them emotionally. While he lost that ability when a sniper's bullet stole his sight, he never lost the knowledge of how to do it. And he passed that knowledge to his children.

Like my father, others have used art to convey ideas, stir emotions, and move people to (1) buy a product or service, (2) learn a new concept or idea, (3) communicate with peers, and (4) transfer knowledge. And it is that principle, sharing what one knows through art, that we will explore in this book.

Knowledge transfer (KT) is not new. Oh, sure, there has been a lot of hub bub around KT over the past 50 years or so, as the college graduates from such prestigious universities as *Yale*, *Harvard*, and *Princeton*, which lead many of the nation's top businesses, began to realize their precious corporations were going to fail if they did not find a way to retain the knowledge locked up inside the heads of their soon-to-be-retired experts – just common sense to us but something these "graduates" had to hire teams of experts and spend millions of dollars in consultation fees to "discover." How sad.

I have never understood why it is that a corporation ignores its own experts only to spend millions of dollars to bring in "experts" to tell them what their own experts have already told them. In fact, my experience is that the outside "experts" come into the organization and spend weeks interviewing the organization's experts, asking them for the solution to the problem, only to include that very same solution as ***the*** solution in the report they finally deliver weeks and sometimes months after completing the investigative part of their contract. And of course, they charge millions of dollars to the organization for that privilege. And that is *legal*!?

One benefit to come out of that widely accepted scam is the need for the organization's experts to transfer their knowledge to those who come after them. That led to the creation of knowledge transfer programs, which, in turn, led to the creation of professional training and development departments within the organization. And that led to you discovering this book!

As an educator or training and development professional, you know the importance of keeping your audience – your learners – engaged in their learning activities. As a lifelong learner, you know that many, many, many learning activities are **boring**! And the last thing you want to do is sit through hours upon hours of mundane content.

No, you would rather *enjoy* your learning activities, which is one reason why virtual worlds and 3D online gaming have taken the world by storm. Researchers, such as Gee (Gee 2005), quickly discovered that computer games provided learning scenarios that could be adapted to real life. For example, *World of Warcraft*, a very popular massively multiplayer online role-playing game, played by millions of people around the world, teaches teamwork, critical thinking and reasoning, reading comprehension, mathematics and statistics, spatial reasoning, how to behave in different cultural settings, perseverance pays off (practice makes perfect), and many other real-life skills. And it teaches all that in a fun, engaging virtual environment that keeps learners coming back time after time and spending their hard-earned money for the privilege.

Academics, too, have known the benefit of using games to engage learners. I remember my elementary school teachers using games as a reward for learning whatever activity my teachers had planned for that day. In fact, Mrs. Zipperson, my second-grade teacher, used the games of *bingo* and *hangman* to teach spelling. Mr. Harvey, my fifth-grade teacher, used an autoharp and songs to teach vocabulary. And of course, our physical education teachers used games to ensure our developing bodies received the exercise they needed (shhh, do not let the kids know their "fun" equals "exercise"!).

These examples support the idea that engagement and interactivity are necessary if we want our learners to continue in their development. However, it is beyond the budget for most companies – especially the smaller ones – to hire teams of game developers, artists, voice-over actors, audio engineers, and musicians to design and launch computer games designed to teach their employees the many skills they must have to ensure the company's success.

So what can those companies do to provide adequate training while keeping their employees engaged?

Is the term *Death by PowerPoint* familiar to you? Generally accepted to have been coined by Angela Garber (Garber 2001), Death by PowerPoint is the phrase used to represent the most acceptable method of torture used by corporations the world over – making their employees sit through hours upon hours of boring, poorly designed visual presentations, usually created in a presentation medium such as Microsoft PowerPoint®.

PowerPoint, Prezi, and other presentation software have been used to create everything from sales pitches to academic lectures, business dashboards, and ineffective instructional content delivered via organizational Learning Management Systems (LMS). It is almost as if the developers of the currently available presentation software were sadists in their past lives…. While PowerPoint does have its uses when its presentations are designed properly, it has been overused. I recommend those training and development professionals serious about engaging their learners and transferring knowledge quickly, consider other options available to them.

One such option is the focus of this book: *Mental Canvas*.

Mental Canvas is the brainchild of a team of researchers at Yale University. Led by Julie Dorsey, the *Frederick W. Beinecke Professor of Computer Science* (Mental Canvas 2016–2022), the team has created an application that takes drawing to a whole new level! No longer are artists and graphics arts professionals limited to static two-dimensional drawings that present information in one plane. Using Mental Canvas, artists can now elevate their art to present their ideas in fun and imaginative ways!

Mental Canvas comes with a set of drawing tools familiar to artists, allowing them to create on any touch screen device with an active pen.[1] Using layers, similar to those used in Adobe Photoshop®, GIMP, and similar software, artists can now present their ideas in a three-dimensional world. Using hinges, they can hide information, allowing users to manipulate the scene to reveal that information. Because the canvas is infinite, artists can create scenes with panoramic views, allowing their users to navigate through the scene, discovering information as they journey through it. Think of it as a poor man's 3D virtual world – without the need for programming expertise!

As we journey through this book together, I will explain each feature of the Mental Canvas application and provide practical exercises that will allow you to quickly develop your skills and expertise with the software's tools.

I will also suggest real-world use applications so that you may quickly develop engaging interactive presentations for use within your organization's training and development programs.

Finally, you will hear from three of the winners of the competition Mental Canvas held for various categories of use. They explain, In His/Her Own Words, how they came to use Mental Canvas and what their experience has been.

The conventions used to explain the material are similar to other such books. The body of the text will be written just as the preceding paragraphs are written.

The In His/Her Own Words sections will be presented on their own separate pages, while the objectives and practical exercises will be offset in separate boxes, allowing you to differentiate them from the body of the book.

---

[1] Note: At this time, Mental Canvas is only available on Microsoft® touch screen devices with active pen and Apple's 3rd and 4th generation iPad Pros with Apple Pencil. Older generations of iPad Pro and other Apple iOS devices may be able to run the application. Also, some PCs running Windows 10 or higher may also be able to run the software. Mental Canvas is not yet available for Android devices. A full list of compatible devices may be accessed by visiting the following website: https://mentalcanvas.com/faq#recommended-hardware

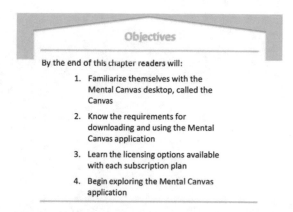

Figure 1. *Example objectives information text box*

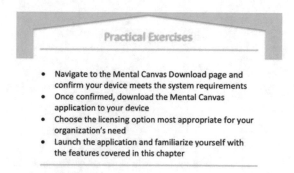

Figure 2. *Example practical exercises information text box*

It is my sincere hope that you will find Mental Canvas as fun and exciting as I have. So, without further delay, let us begin the journey!

Bibliography

Garber, Angela. April 1, 2001. *Death by PowerPoint.* www.smallbusinesscomputing.com/software/death-by-powerpoint/.

Gee, J.P. 2005. "Good Video Games and Good Learning." *Phi Kappa Phi Forum* (The Honor Society of Phi Kappa Phi) 85 (2): 33–37.

Mental Canvas. 2016–2022. *The Mental Canvas Story.* https://mentalcanvas.com/about.

SECTION I

Overview

CHAPTER 1

Overview of Mental Canvas

Mental Canvas was created as a result of research conducted by a team at Yale University led by Dr. Julie Dorsey, the Frederick W. Beinecke Professor of Computer Science. The team's mission was to bring drawing on digital devices into the 21st century, changing the way we think of creating artwork forever (Mental Canvas 2016–2022). No longer would creatives be limited to static two-dimensional (2D) images.

Rather, using the Mental Canvas application, they are able to create 2D with a three-dimensional (3D) aspect capable of being scrolled, panned, and exported to the Web as video fly-throughs and with which we can interact.[1]

This chapter will provide an overview of Mental Canvas fundamentals that will be used in the rest of the book. The objectives of this chapter are as follows.

---

[1] Interactive video fly-throughs are available using the web player on the Mental Canvas website.

M. Commini, *Mental Canvas for Training and Development*,
https://doi.org/10.1007/978-1-4842-8774-3_1

Objectives

By the end of this chapter readers will:

1. Familiarize themselves with the Mental Canvas desktop, called the Canvas

2. Know the requirements for downloading and using the Mental Canvas application

3. Learn the licensing options available with each subscription plan

4. Begin exploring the Mental Canvas application

The Mental Canvas files can be edited cross-platform, used by teams for collaboration, shared with colleagues, or created and edited by single users. According to the Mental Canvas website, using the application allows creatives to

- Create quick animations (called Animatics by the Mental Canvas team)

- Uncover and hide details

- Show elements in context

- Change viewpoints

- Annotate and elaborate

- Reuse, refine, and adapt elements of a drawing

- Mix media, photos, graphic art, and drawing (Mental Canvas 2016–2022)

Essentially, the end product is "an interactive, immersive spatial drawing" (Dorsey and Nassour, 2021).

By editing exported videos with computer software such as *Adobe Premiere Pro*®, *iMovie*®, and similar postproduction applications, audio tracks can be added, giving your videos another way of interacting with your clients. By using software such as TechSmith Corporation's *Camtasia*®, it is possible to add text box pop-ups, audio tracks, and URL hotspots.[2]

The Mental Canvas application is available on the Mental Canvas website: `https://mentalcanvas.com` (see Figure 1-1). Currently, it is only designed for use on Windows® and iOS® devices. The Mental Canvas team is exploring porting the application to Android devices, but at the time of this writing, it cannot be used on the Android platform (Mental Canvas 2016–2021).[3]

Requirements

To be able to download and run the Mental Canvas application, you must have a touch device running Windows 10 and an active pen. iOS users must have an iPad Pro 3rd or 4th generation and an Apple Pencil. Figure 1-1 shows an example of the download screen on the Mental Canvas website.

---

[2] Adobe Premiere Pro®, iMovie®, and Camtasia® are registered trademarks of Adobe, Apple Inc., and TechSmith Corporation, respectively.

[3] Windows® and iOS® are registered trademarks of Microsoft Corporation and Apple Inc., respectively.

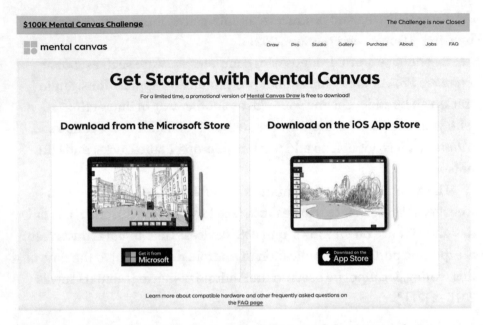

Figure 1-1. *The download page on the Mental Canvas website*

Licensing

Figure 1-2 shows the licensing options for the Mental Canvas application. Available options are dependent upon which license you select.

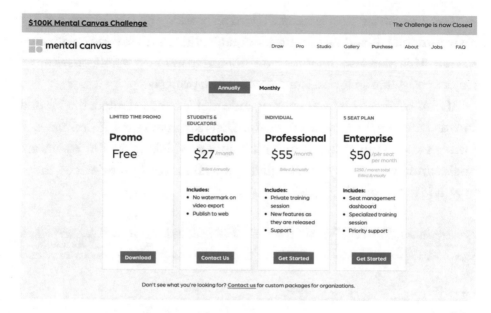

Figure 1-2. *The Mental Canvas licensing options*

The **Promo** license is free to use; however, *Publish to Web* is not available, and videos are watermarked on export. How long this license will remain available has not been announced by the Mental Canvas team.

Figure 1-3 shows a comparison between the remaining plans. The recently announced **Creator** plan is available for a one-time purchase fee. Currently, the plan only allows for one public interactive web scene and does not include new features or private training.

As can be seen, the only difference between the **Education** plan and the other plans is the amount of training and support available to the end user.

The **Professional** plan can be used by individual creatives working alone or with other creatives also holding a Professional plan license. It is suitable for small organizations with one or two creatives on staff.

The **Enterprise** plan is for use by teams working in a collaborative environment. It is suitable for larger organizations with several creatives on staff. This plan also includes a dashboard to manage seat licenses and project consultation for assistance with team projects.

If none of these plans fit your organization's needs, contact the Mental Canvas team and inquire about custom licensing packages. A *Contact us* link is provided under the license plan options. Clicking the link opens an email window in your system's email application. For Apple devices, the default is the Apple Mail app.

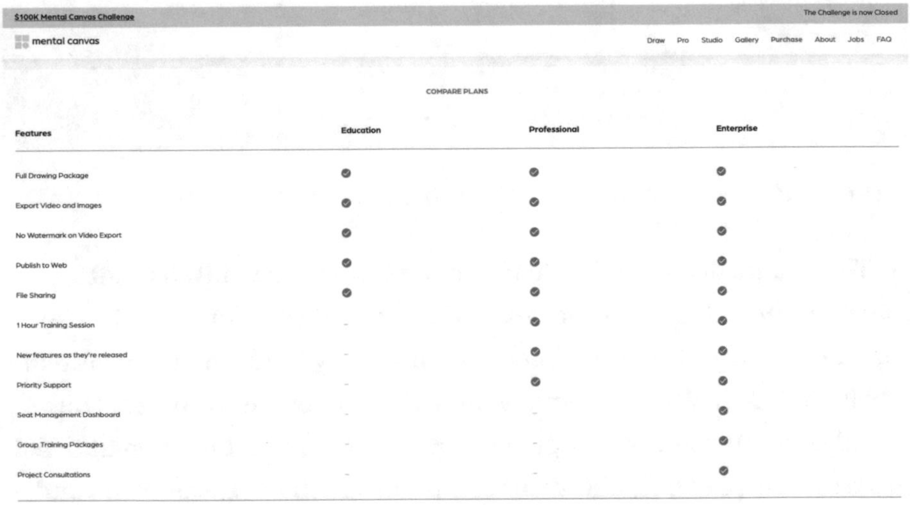

Figure 1-3. *Mental Canvas subscription plan comparison*

There is one other option available that any organization can utilize, but that may be especially appropriate for those organizations without creatives on staff. Mental Canvas Studio (see Figure 1-4) allows the end user to contact the Mental Canvas team for the creation of custom content. Their team of creatives will, for a price, take an organization's project idea from concept to finished media. Contact with the Mental Canvas Studio team is possible by visiting the Mental Canvas website, clicking the link for *Studio*, and scrolling down to the bottom of the web page. I do not know what the response time is.[4]

Figure 1-4. *Mental Canvas Studio*

A Closer Look at Mental Canvas

In the following sections, we will begin our exploration of the Mental Canvas application. This includes launching the application, device orientation, the Viewing and Drawing modes, and common elements between the views.

---

[4] **Disclaimer:** Other than as an end user of the Mental Canvas application, I am not affiliated with Mental Canvas or any of its team members.

Launching Mental Canvas

When you launch the Mental Canvas app on your device, you are presented with the Splash Screen (see Figure 1-5).

Figure 1-5. *The Mental Canvas Splash Screen*

Once the application has opened, you will be presented with the canvas view (see Figures 1-6 and 1-7). In this case, my scene opened in the Drawing mode.

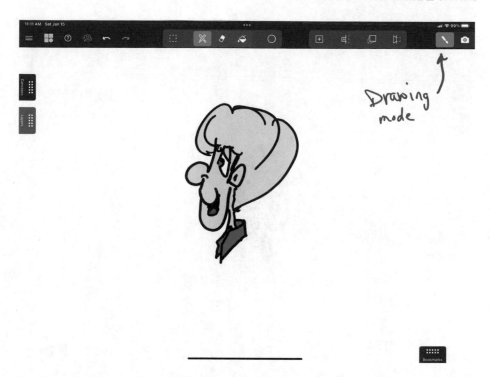

Figure 1-6. *Mental Canvas Drawing mode*

Figure 1-7. *Mental Canvas Viewing mode*

As you can see in Figures 1-6 and 1-7, the Canvas has two main modes: the Drawing and Viewing modes. Each mode has its own set of tools (see Figure 1-8).

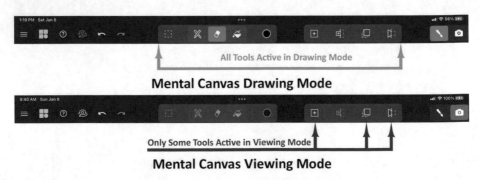

Figure 1-8. *The active tools based on mode selection*

We will deep dive into the toolbar for the Drawing and Viewing modes in later chapters. For now, we will explore the views' common elements and device orientation.

Orientation

By now, you know that the Mental Canvas application can be used on either a Windows multi-touch-screen device with an active pen or an Apple iPad Pro with an Apple Pencil. One of the nice features of these devices is the ability to use them in either the Portrait or Landscape mode, allowing creatives to draw and paint however they are most comfortable.

As you can see in Figure 1-9, Mental Canvas allows you to take advantage of whichever orientation you prefer. Of course, in Portrait mode, you do not have as much drawing real estate as you do in Landscape mode. But since the canvas is unlimited, you are not really restricted.

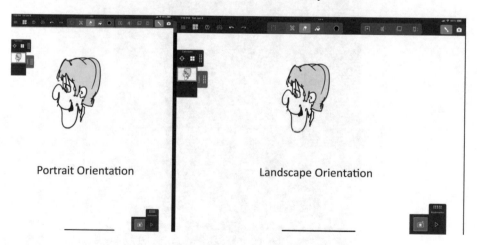

Figure 1-9. *Mental Canvas allows you to use your preferred orientation*

The Views' Common Elements

As you have been following along, you will have noticed the toolbars for
each view share common elements (Figure 1-10). They are as follows, from
left to right:

≡ The hamburger icon – Clicking on this icon opens the Mental
Canvas menu where you can add scenes, view video tutorials, save your
file, export videos and screenshots, publish to the Web (not available when
using the free promo license), view scene info, and access system settings.
We will explore the menu further in other sections of the book.

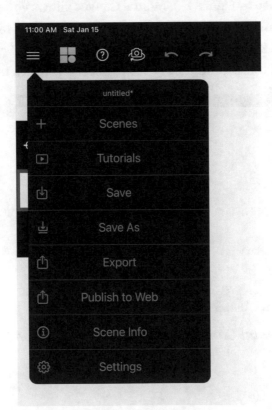

Figure 1-10. *The Mental Canvas menu*

The Mental Canvas logo icon – Clicking on this icon opens the Mental Canvas license screen (Figure 1-11). This screen shows the subscription plan you are on and your login username and provides a link to the release notes and a link to support. You will also notice at the very bottom the software libraries in use with the Mental Canvas application.

Figure 1-11. *The Mental Canvas license screen*

The Help menu icon – Clicking on this icon will open a list of the available tutorial videos (Figure 1-12). According to a recent communication with the Mental Canvas support team (Mental Canvas Support, 2022), the videos were shot on a Windows Surface tablet using an active pen. Windows users reading this book can refer to the videos to explore any features that are not the same between the Surface and iPad Pro devices.

Although most features are similar between the two devices, according to the support team in that email, "sometimes we release a feature on one platform before the other, and there are other platform-specific requirements, so they're not identical."

Figure 1-12. *Some of the tutorial videos available through the Help menu*

The Undo icon – Users of word processing and other software applications will recognize this icon. Should you make a mistake or decide you want to take your creative in a different direction, clicking on this icon will undo the previous step. From my experience, you can undo over 100 steps.

The Redo icon – Similar to the Undo function, clicking on this icon will redo the steps you undid. So if you decide that you really did want to do something you undid, clicking this icon will bring that step back.

In addition to the shared common elements on the toolbars, you will have noticed three panels that remain available to the end user regardless of which canvas view they have selected (Figure 1-13). Those panels will be covered more in depth later. They are as follows:

- The Canvas Panel

- The Layers Panel

- The Bookmarks Panel

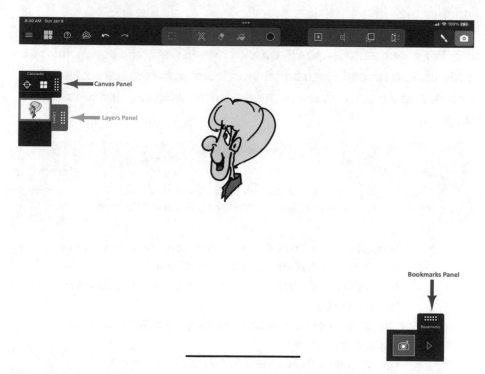

Figure 1-13. *The Canvas, Layers, and Bookmarks Panels*

Summary

In this chapter, we began exploring the Mental Canvas application for certain touch devices. Developed by researchers to allow creatives to add animations, interactivity, and 3D conceptualizations to 2D digital artwork, Mental Canvas can be used in either portrait or landscape orientation on Windows® and iOS® touch devices using an active pen or Apple Pencil.

Readers learned what the system requirements are for downloading and using the Mental Canvas application as well as the different subscription licensing options available to the end user.

Finally, we began exploring the Mental Canvas application and learned the common elements available to us in the two canvas modes: Drawing and Viewing.

In Chapter 2, we will explore creating a scene and managing scene files. Beginning with Chapter 3, we will cover in depth the inner workings of Mental Canvas and begin building an interactive computer safety presentation for use with the organization's training and development program.

Practical Exercises

- Navigate to the Mental Canvas Download page and confirm your device meets the system requirements
- Once confirmed, download the Mental Canvas application to your device
- Choose the licensing option most appropriate for your organization's need
- Launch the application and familiarize yourself with the features covered in this chapter

Bibliography

Dorsey, Julie, and Sam Nassour. 2021. *Mental Canvas: Drawing Reimagined - Lightbox Expo 2021*. September 13. https://www.youtube.com/watch?v=QoZe8CHW5jc.

Gallagher, Tyler. 2021. *Meet The Inventors: Julie Dorsey of Mental Canvas On How To Go From Idea To Store Shelf (Question 1)*. September 23. Accessed March 4, 2022. https://medium.com/p/f327105d3922.

Mental Canvas. 2016–2021. *Frequently Asked Questions.* https://mentalcanvas.com/faq.

Mental Canvas. 2016–2021. *Mental Canvas expands drawing and enhances expression.* https://mentalcanvas.com/pro.

Mental Canvas. 2022. *Mental Canvas in the News.* Accessed 03 04, 2022. https://mentalcanvas.com/company/press.

Mental Canvas Support. 2022. *Personal Communication via email.* January 13.

Mental Canvas. 2016–2021. *The Mental Canvas Story.* https://mentalcanvas.com/about.

Mental Canvas: The Origin Story

As you sit reading this page, visualize yourself as a creative individual, having played in your sandbox as a child, building wonderful things as your imagination dreamed them up. Encouraged by your parents, you spent years creating and building – exploring your world as only a creative can.

Now, imagine years later you are studying architecture, thinking this will be your life's work when you visit a computer lab and discover a world of 3D images and you realize the computers in this lab have been used to create and manage those images. And this fascinates you! Suddenly, your passion for architecture is no longer your primary focus. Rather, you discover a love for computers and how they can enhance the world around us. The same world you explored as a child!

According to an *Interview with Tyler Gallagher*, published in *Authority Magazine*, a *Medium* publication (Gallagher 2021), that is what happened to Dr. Julie Dorsey, founder and chief scientist at Mental Canvas, Inc., and the *Frederick W. Beinecke Professor of Computer Science* at Yale University. When she realized mathematics could be used to create and control the 3D images she saw on the computer display, her mind began playing with the many possibilities this presented.

Years later, after graduating with a PhD in computer science with a specialization in computer graphics, she realized "that despite all the progress, designs still begin on paper" (Gallagher 2021). She knew there had to be a way to use computers to enhance computer drawing, to bring it into the 21st century – changing it forever from the limitations of drawing on paper.

So she did what any self-respecting scientist does and applied for, and received, a grant through the National Science Foundation. The funding from the grant allowed her to conduct the research necessary to attain her goals. Interested readers can find her published results on the Yale University website.[5, 6]

The results from her research provided the opportunity for her to receive additional grants, which made it possible for her to move Mental Canvas out of the laboratory and commercialize it for the benefit of society as a whole (Gallagher 2021).[7] To date, Mental Canvas generated awards and accolades any inventor may be proud of (Mental Canvas 2022).

---

[5] https://graphics.cs.yale.edu/publications/mental-canvas-tool-conceptual-architectural-design-and-analysis

[6] https://graphics.cs.yale.edu/publications/sketching-reality-realistic-interpretation-architectural-designs

[7] Additional source material *(Mental Canvas Ushers Drawing Into A New Dimension)*: www.prnewswire.com/news-releases/mental-canvas-ushers-drawing-into-a-new-dimension-300351779.html and (Q&A with Julie Dorsey: Yale Faculty Founder of Mental Canvas): https://city.yale.edu/stories/2017/9/26/qa-with-julie-dorsey-yale-faculty-founder-of-mental-canvas

SECTION II

Your First Scene and Managing Its Files

CHAPTER 2

The Scene and File Management

Now that you are familiar with the basic functions of Mental Canvas discussed in Chapter 1, we will explore the scene, its canvases and layers, and file management. The scene is the finished product – the container that holds your creation, if you will. The staff at Mental Canvas call it "a spatial drawing" (Mental Canvas, 2021).

Objectives

By the end of this chapter readers will be able to:

a. Create new scenes

b. Save their scenes

c. Perform File Management functions

© Michael Commini 2023
M. Commini, *Mental Canvas for Training and Development*,
https://doi.org/10.1007/978-1-4842-8774-3_2

File Management Overview

Before we begin working with Mental Canvas to produce our creatives, a brief explanation of the file management system is in order. A more in-depth look will occur as we complete each section.

When you install the Mental Canvas app onto your device, a Mental Canvas folder is created inside your device's file management system. Figure 2-1 shows the created folder on an iPad Pro. By default, your files are created and saved inside that folder.

It is possible to create, save, edit, and delete scenes in other folders including external drives. We will explore that topic further later in this chapter.

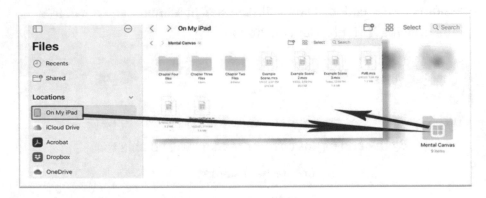

Figure 2-1. *File management overview*

Creating New Scenes

Made up of canvases and layers, each project can have only one scene but can have multiple canvases and layers. As we move through this chapter together, we will learn how to create a scene and progress to adding canvases and layers.

Begin by launching your Mental Canvas application on either your iPad Pro 3rd or 4th generation or Windows multi-touch device. I will be working with my iPad Pro 3rd gen and using my Apple Pencil. The principles and concepts are similar enough between iOS and Windows devices that Windows users should have no difficulty following along.

As stated in Chapter 1, the Mental Canvas files can be edited cross-platform, used by teams for collaboration, shared with colleagues, or created and edited by single users. As we work with our files, I will explain how.

From within your Mental Canvas scene, click on the hamburger menu to open the file management menu (Figure 2-2). We will only cover the basic functions in this chapter. We will cover the more advanced menu selections in a later chapter. Click on the + *Scenes* option to make a scene (Figure 2-3).

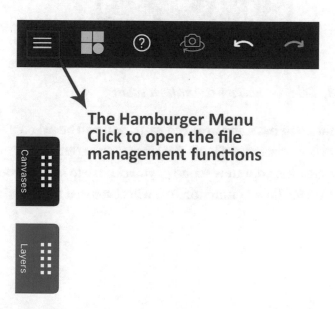

Figure 2-2. *The hamburger menu allows access to the file management functions*

Figure 2-3. *Select + Scenes to make a scene*

Note that if you have any unsaved work, you will be asked if you
want to save it or discard it (Figure 2-4). Select the appropriate answer
to continue creating your new scene (if you choose to save it, you will be
taken into the *File Save As* function. We will cover that function later in this
chapter).

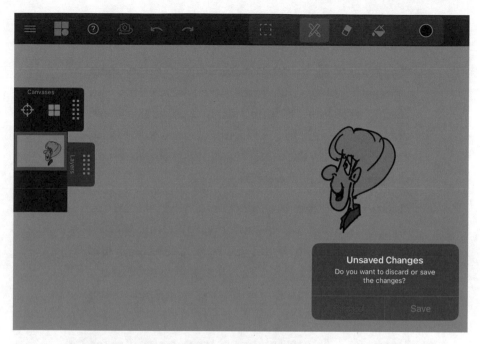

Figure 2-4. *Unsaved changes prompt*

Refer to Figure 2-5 for this next section: a new window will open showing your device's file structure. Choose a location for your new scene. The default is the Mental Canvas folder, but you can select any location you want. If you are following along, choose the Mental Canvas folder. The next window that opens will present you with two choices by which you can create your scene. You can click on the + sign next to the new folder icon at the top of the window, or click on the icon that looks like a piece of paper with a plus sign in its center. Clicking on either icon will open another window, allowing you to choose from one of the templates on the Templates tab. Your choices at the time of this writing are as follows:

- Blank – This template allows you to create a new blank scene.

- Foreground Midground Background – This template opens with several canvases already started for you. Each canvas has a different starting point. If you are comfortable with your skills or just want to jump right in and play with the app, this template starts you off completely blank. Go for it!

- Room – This template starts you off as if you are on stage or in a box with the front wall missing. It includes canvases for the floor, ceiling, back of the room, and your left and right walls. This template would be a good place to begin for an office or academic setting representation.

- Panorama – This template includes a series of canvases that represent one point on the compass – North, South, East, West, and points in between. This would be great for an art studio creating a virtual fly-through of the pieces it has on display.

- Cube – Are you old enough to remember those picture cubes that were all the rage in the 1980s? This template starts you off with six walls of a cube. You can place any content you want on each wall: top, bottom, right, left, front, back. This template would be suitable for just about anything – even as a virtual picture cube!

Note   If you decide not to create a scene, simply click anywhere outside the templates window to close it and return to the previous window. To return to the current scene, click Done.

Except for the blank template, the templates contain a layer with guides – lines delineating the area inside which you may place your content. Of course, since the canvases are infinite, you can place your content literally anywhere you desire!

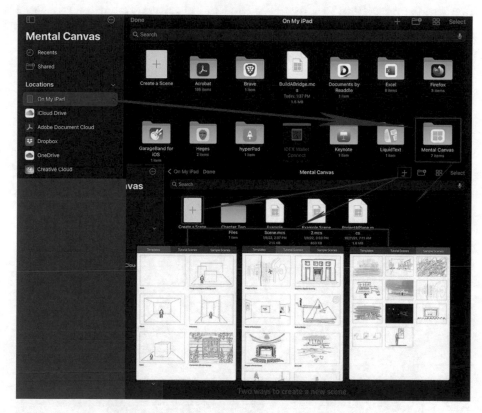

Figure 2-5. *Creating a scene: choosing your template*

Once you have selected the template you wish to use, you will be required to name it. You can use the default name, Scene, or you can give it a name that makes sense for your project. As you can see in Figure 2-6, I have chosen to name the scene after one of the characters in my children's books. You may have noticed that Harvey's profile has been used in some of the examples in Chapters 1 and 2. You will see more of Harvey as you progress through the book.

As the scene is created by the software, it is placed in whichever location you chose when you began the scene creation process. Figure 2-7 shows you an example of where the Harvey Rumplemeyer scene is located. You will use this location any time you wish to open this scene. The file location is on the iPad Pro, inside of the Mental Canvas, Chapter Two Files folder. Notice the scene file name ends in the file name extension .mcs. Want to take a guess what .mcs stands for?

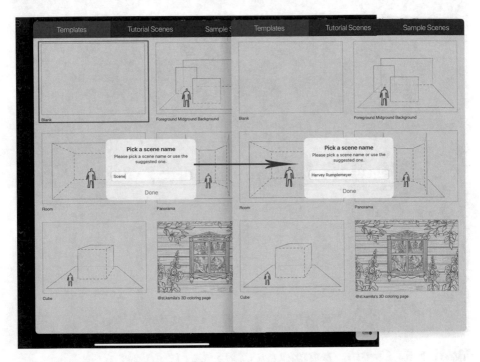

Figure 2-6. *You will be required to give your scene a name*

Figure 2-7. *The scene file location*

If you make a mistake in naming your scene, or you decide later to delete it, with your finger or your pen/pencil, press and hold the file's icon. A new menu will open (see Figure 2-8) that will allow you to complete several functions. They include the following:

- Renaming your file – You will rename the file using the same procedure your system normally uses.

- Deleting your file – Immediately removes the file and sends it to the system trash can/recycle bin. *Be careful*, you are not prompted to confirm the deletion. If you accidentally delete a file without realizing you have done so, you will drive yourself crazy looking for it. Remember this advice and look in your trash. Recover the file just as you would normally on your device.

- Duplicate – Immediately makes a second copy of your file and appends a sequential number at the end of the file name (before the file name extension). This is useful if you want to use some components of the file for another project.

- Tags – On the iPad Pro, you can add tags to your file. This is useful for knowledge management and search activities. A similar function may be available on Windows devices.

- Copy – This places a copy of the file on your device's clipboard, which allows you to paste the file into another location. You can also paste it into an email to send to a colleague as long as the file size is not outside the allowable range of your email client.

- Get info – Allows you to examine your file's metadata.

- Share – This function allows you to place a copy of the scene on an external drive, such as the company intranet, for retrieval by colleagues and collaborators.

Figure 2-8. *Available file management functions*

Saving Your Scene

Just as with other computer software with which you are familiar, you must periodically save your work. Failing to do so means you will lose hours upon hours of your creative effort. The developers at Mental Canvas have made saving your work a very simple process and given us two different ways to save. Please refer to Figure 2-9.

The first method allows you to make your initial file save. To perform this task, click on the hamburger menu and select *Save As*. A new window will open, allowing you to either save your work in the original location established when you created your scene or save your file somewhere else, such as an external drive or another location on your device. Figure 2-10 is an example of what you will see.

From this window, you can rename your scene, choose the location in which to save your file, choose to create a new folder into which your file will be saved, and cancel the save to return to your current scene. Figures 2-11 and 2-12 provide examples of what you will see when creating a new folder into which your scene files will be placed.

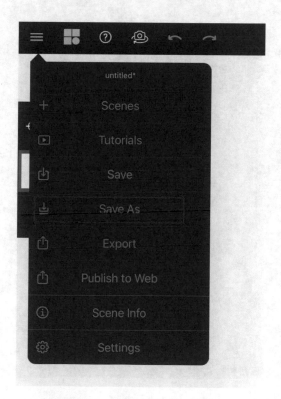

Figure 2-9. *Using the Save As function to perform your initial file save*

Navigate to the location in which you will place your new folder and click the new folder icon 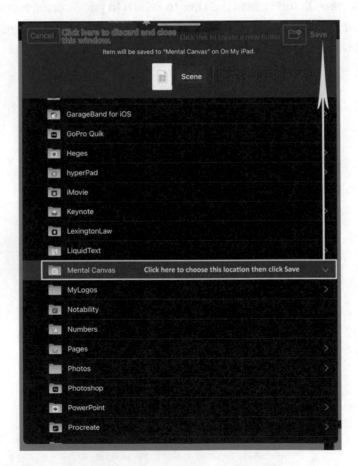 to open the new folder window. Here, you can give your new folder a name by double-clicking in the text box that says *untitled folder*. Windows users should use the naming convention provided with their Windows 10+ software. Click *Done* when finished. Should you decide you do not want the new folder, simply click *Cancel* to return to the previous window. From here, you can either choose a new location or click *Cancel* again to return to the current scene.

Figure 2-10. *The File Save As option*

Note   The aforementioned procedure is what you will experience when using the *File Save As* function of the hamburger menu. Your experience will be slightly different should you choose to create a new folder while creating a new scene. In that instance, clicking the new folder icon will immediately create a new *untitled folder*. You can name that folder if you wish or leave it untitled. To remove any folder you no longer want, simply press and hold on the folder until the submenu pops up (refer back to Figure 2-8). Then choose *Delete* to send the folder to the *Recycle Bin*.

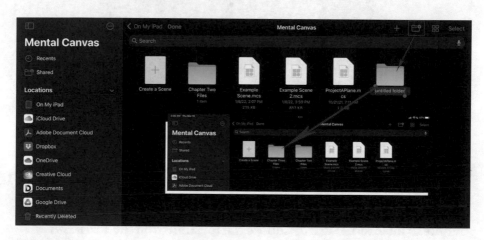

Figure 2-11. *Making a new folder*

Figure 2-12. *Naming your new folder*

The same *Save As* process can be followed should you choose to save your file to an external drive. Choose the location from the *Locations* sidebar menu on your iPad Pro. Create new folders as needed. Windows users choose the appropriate location provided by the Windows 10+ software.

Once you have performed your first file save, you can use the second method of saving to periodically save your work (see Figure 2-13). ***Note:*** Currently, Mental Canvas *does not* have an autosave feature. If you do not periodically save your work, you will lose whatever content you have created since your last save when you close out of the application.

I recommend if you are not already in the habit of doing so, you get into the habit of saving your work at least once every 20 minutes. Doing so could mean you never have to experience the frustration millions of end users the world over have felt when the power went out and their computers shut down causing them to lose hours upon hours of work.

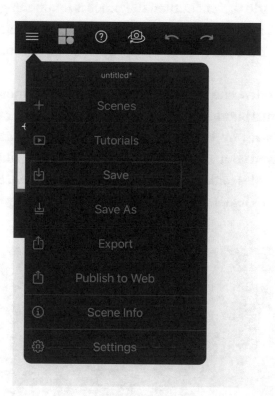

Figure 2-13. *Periodically save your work with the Save function*

Closing the Application

As with every iOS application, dragging your finger up from the bottom of the application will close the application. Should you have any unsaved changes at the time you close the app, you will not be prompted to save them. Rather, you will find them ready and waiting the next time you launch the Mental Canvas application.

Opening Your Scene

To open your scene, first, launch the Mental Canvas application. You will experience one of two scenarios: (1) you will open to a blank canvas or (2) you will open to the previous scene/canvas with which you were working. Whichever scenario you encounter, the process for opening scenes is the same. Of course, it goes without saying that if your application opened to the scene with which you wish to work, you need do nothing but begin working.

To choose your scene, first, click on the hamburger menu and then select the + Scenes button. You will be prompted to save any unsaved changes if you have any. Your window will open to the last scene location to which you saved your work. If this is your first time, it will open to the default, iPad Pro files folder, *On My iPad* (see Figure 2-15). From there, tap the *Mental Canvas* folder to open it. Locate the scene file you want and tap it to open it.

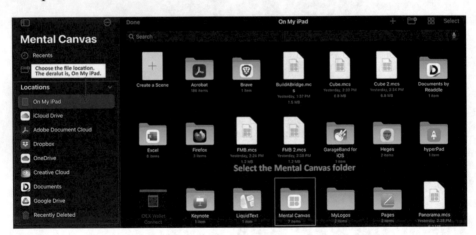

Figure 2-14. *Choose the file location*

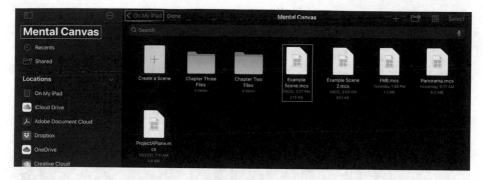

Figure 2-15. *Tap to open the scene file*

The scene will open to your canvas, and you can proceed to draw from there.

Additional File Management Functions

Besides being able to right-click on a file and open a submenu that allows you to perform file maintenance, as seen in Figure 2-8, the Mental Canvas developers have provided a secondary method for performing some of the same tasks. Refer to Figure 2-16 for this next section.

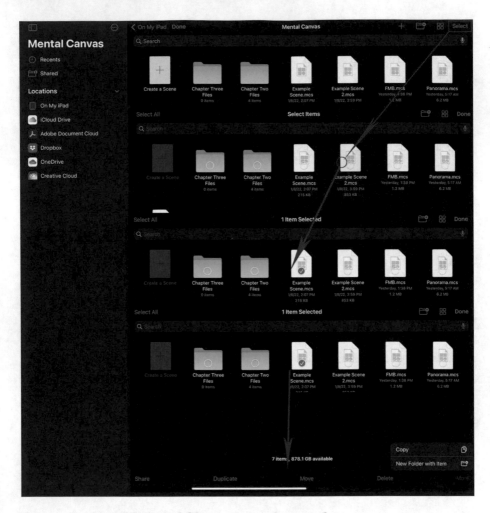

Figure 2-16. *Additional file management tools*

Tap + Scenes to open the files folder. Tap the word *Select* in the top right corner of the window. Immediately after tapping on *Select,* the window will change slightly. Where the word *Select* was is now the word *Done*. At the top left of the new window are the words *Select All*, which allows you to select all of the files in view. And once you have selected one or more files to manage, at the bottom of the window, you will find the file management submenu:

- Share – Allows you to share your scene files with teammates

- Duplicate – Creates a duplicate of your scene

- Move – Allows you to move your file to a new location

- Delete – Allows you to delete your file and send it to the Recycle Bin

- More – Tapping on More will open an additional submenu:

    - Copy – Allows you to copy the file

    - New Folder with Item – Allows you to create a new folder that contains the file you have selected

- Tapping *Done* when you have completed your tasks takes you back to the previous window. Tapping *Done* again takes you back into your current scene.

And finally, the developers have provided a way for you to sort your files in three different views (see Figure 2-17): Icons, List, and Columns. Once you have chosen your preferred view, you can then sort by Name, Kind, Date, Size, Tags, or Use Groups.

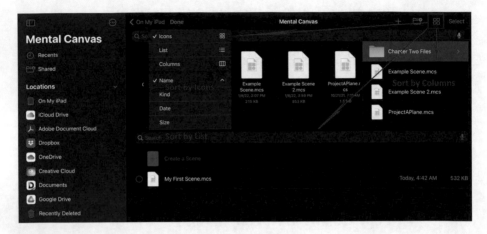

Figure 2-17. *The different file views for sorting*

Summary

In this chapter, I have tried to be as comprehensive as possible regarding scene creation and the management of scene files. I have shown you how to create a scene, where to save that scene, how to access and open that scene, and then the various file management tools and functions available to Mental Canvas users. In later chapters, we will explore the remaining hamburger menu choices: Tutorials, Export, Publish to Web (not available for free license users), Scene Info, and Settings.

Beginning in Chapter 3, we will explore the Drawing View, the Canvas and Layers Panels, and the various Drawing View tools available to us.

Practical Exercises

Launch Mental Canvas and create your first scene
Using the file management tools:

- Name your scene and save it to a location of your choosing
- Make a copy of your scene and paste it in a new location
- Share your scene with a colleague
- Move your scene to a different location
- Delete the scene file and recover it

Bibliography

Dorsey, Julie, and Sam Nassour. 2021. *Mental Canvas: Drawing Reimagined – Lightbox Expo 2021.* September 13. www.youtube.com/watch?v=QoZe8CHW5jc.

Gallagher, Tyler. 2021. *Meet The Inventors: Julie Dorsey of Mental Canvas On How To Go From Idea To Store Shelf (Question 1).* September 23. Accessed March 4, 2022. https://medium.com/p/f327105d3922.

— Authority Magazine. 2021. *Meet The Inventors: Julie Dorsey of Mental Canvas On How To Go From Idea To Store Shelf (Question 4).* September 23. Accessed March 4, 2022. https://medium.com/p/f327105d3922.

— Authority Magazine. 2021. *Meet The Inventors: Julie Dorsey of Mental Canvas On How To Go From Idea To Store Shelf (Question 5).* September 23. Accessed March 4, 2022. https://medium.com/p/f327105d3922.

Mental Canvas. 2016–2021. *Frequently Asked Questions.* https://mentalcanvas.com/faq.

—Mental Canvas. 2021. *Get Started Drawing.* October 4. Accessed 2022. `https://youtu.be/MGpOID7PxDw`.

—Mental Canvas. 2016–2021. *Mental Canvas expands drawing and enhances expression.* `https://mentalcanvas.com/pro`.

—Mental Canvas. 2022. *Mental Canvas in the News.* Accessed March 4, 2022. `https://mentalcanvas.com/company/press`.

Mental Canvas Support. January 13, 2022. *Personal communication via email.*

Mental Canvas. 2016–2021. *The Mental Canvas Story.* `https://mentalcanvas.com/about`.

CHAPTER 3

The Drawing Mode: The Basics

If you are like me, as soon as you have your copy of Mental Canvas downloaded and installed on your device, and your first scene created, you are going to want to begin exploring. That is, after all, one of the reasons for acquiring this book, right? This chapter is written to help you do just that.

Recall from Chapter 1 that Mental Canvas comes with a set of tools common between the two views. In this chapter, we will explore those tools specific to the *Drawing Mode*. While these tools may be familiar to those readers conversant with similar graphics programs, there are some that will be new to you. And for those readers who have never used graphics software before, this chapter will help put you at ease. Once you see how well the minds behind Mental Canvas designed the software, you will find the learning curve is much faster than other programs, such as Adobe Photoshop®, Adobe Illustrator®, or even Procreate®.[1]

The learning objectives for this chapter are as follows.

---

[1] Photoshop and Illustrator are registered trademarks of Adobe, Inc.; Procreate is a registered trademark of Savage Interactive Pty Ltd.

© Michael Commini 2023
M. Commini, *Mental Canvas for Training and Development*,
https://doi.org/10.1007/978-1-4842-8774-3_3

Objectives

By the end of this chapter readers will know how to use the basic Drawing Mode tools:

a. Selection

b. Brushes

c. Eraser

d. Paint Bucket

e. Color Palette

Getting Started

When you first launch Mental Canvas, it will either open to the last scene you were working with or open to a new, blank, untitled scene. Either way, the first thing you should do once the scene is open is to verify that you are in *Drawing Mode*. You do this by confirming the brush icon in the top right corner of your canvas is on – indicated by its turning blue – and by confirming your drawing tool icons are blue when selected. If the camera icon is orange and your drawing tools are grayed out, you are in *Viewing mode*.[2] (Please see Figures 3-1 and 3-2.)

---

[2] Note that at least one Mental Canvas trainer refers to the Viewing Mode as the Navigation Mode. Either designation is correct as both are used by the Mental Canvas team.

Figure 3-1. *Once Mental Canvas has launched, verify you are in Drawing Mode*

Figure 3-3 shows the drawing tools available to us in the *Drawing Mode*. For the purposes of this book, they are grouped as the *Selection & Art tools* and the *Parallel Projection tools*. While they appear similar to other programs, they are what sets Mental Canvas apart from all other graphics software. They are the engine that drives Mental Canvas. Beginning from the left side of Figure 3-3, we will explore each of the editing and art tools.

Figure 3-2. *An orange camera icon means you are in Viewing Mode*

The Drawing Mode Tools: The Basics

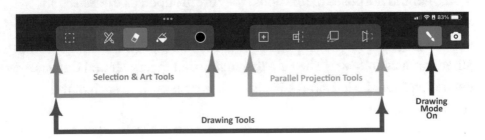

Figure 3-3. *The drawing tools*

Making Selections

The Selection tool – As the name implies, this tool allows the user to make selections to objects on the canvas. To activate, ensure *Drawing Mode* is on and then tap the Selection tool. The canvas will change states[3] and will immediately open to a set of selection and editing tools which we will explore together (please refer to Figure 3-4). To cancel the selection and return to the unselected state at any time, simply tap the Selection tool icon again.

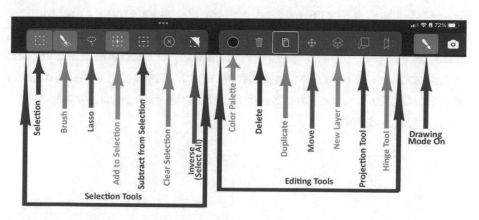

Figure 3-4. *The selection and editing tools*

There are two ways to select and deselect objects on the canvas. You can use the Brush tool, , to swipe over the object (or a portion of the object if you only want to adjust one area), or you can use the Lasso tool, , to draw around the object. You can also use the Lasso tool to draw around a small area of an object if you only want to adjust one part of that object. Figure 3-5 provides examples of each method.

---

[3] Note that when using the selection tools, the canvas has two states: selection on and selection off. Whichever state you are, you are working on the same canvas.

Activate the Add-to-the-Selection tool, , to add to the selection and the Subtract-from-the-Selection tool, , to remove the selection (or portion of the selection).

The Clear Selection tool, , removes the selection. You can then return to the main canvas or reselect another object or region of an object.

The Inverse Selection tool, , changes the selection from the first object you selected to the rest of the canvas. For example, referring to Figure 3-5, if you select the area around the character's mouth and then tap Inverse, the mouth will become deselected while the rest of the character (and any other objects on the canvas) will become selected. The Inverse tool can also be used as a Select-All tool. Try it out: with no objects selected, tap the Inverse tool. Every object on the canvas is now selected and ready for editing!

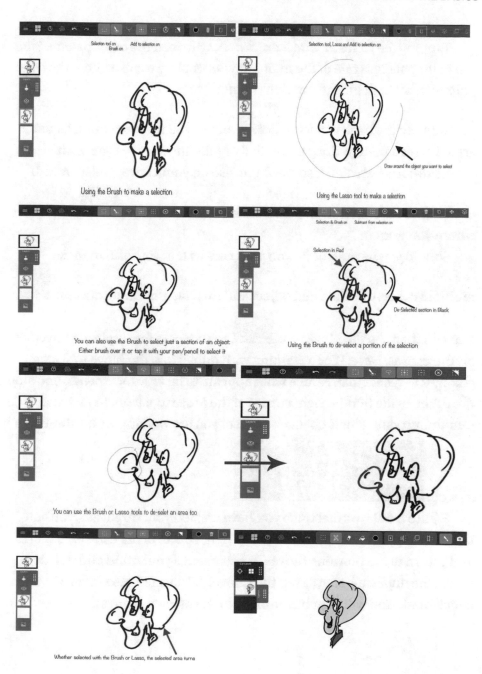

Figure 3-5. *Using the Brush and Lasso tools to select and deselect*

Tapping the Color Palette icon, ████, will open the color palette. Since the color palette is one of the main drawing tools, we will explore the color palette more in depth later in this chapter.

Tapping the trash can icon, 🗑, allows you to delete the selected area. You can then re-draw as needed or edit the object as you wish.

To re-locate an object somewhere else on your canvas, select it with either the brush or lasso and then click on the Move tool, ⊕, to place it where you want it.

Should you have an object on your canvas that you wish to make multiple copies of, select that object and then tap the Duplicate tool, ▢.

You can then use the Move tool, ⊕, to re-locate the duplicate anywhere on the canvas. *Note:* When working with duplicates, the Move tool icon changes to reflect that. Notice what appears to be two documents, one atop the other, in the bottom right corner of the Move tool icon. In fact, the remaining editing tools change to reflect you are working with a duplicate

as well: .

Figure 3-6 shows that once you have created your duplicate, you can tap the Confirm check mark in the top right corner of the canvas to keep it and return to the previous canvas. If you change your mind and decide not to use the duplicate, simply tap the Cancel "X" located next to the Confirm check mark. You will then be returned to the previous canvas.

Figure 3-6. *Making and moving duplicate objects*

Once you have finished making your selections, tap the selection tool once again to return to the main canvas.

The remaining editing tools – New Layer, Parallel Projection, and Hinge – and their associated duplicate versions will be discussed in the next chapter.

Choosing a Brush

As with other graphics software, Mental Canvas comes with an assortment of brushes. To choose a brush and select its size, click on the Brush icon,

. Figure 3-7 shows an example of the Brushes Panel, while Figure 3-8 provides examples of the associated brush strokes.

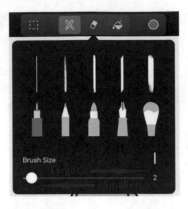

Figure 3-7. *The Brushes Panel*

Currently, there are five brushes: fine point, pencil, marker, calligraphy, and brush. Select the brush with which you want to work. The selected brush is indicated when its associated icon turns blue on the palette. Adjust the brush size using the Brush Size slider. Moving the slider to the right makes your brush size larger and to the left, smaller. Tap anywhere on the canvas or on the Brush tool icon to close the palette and begin drawing. Figure 3-8 shows examples of each brush.

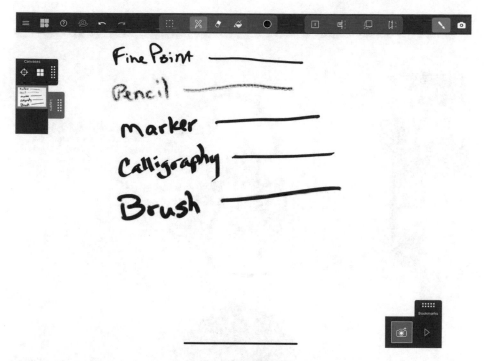

Figure 3-8. *The brushes provided with Mental Canvas*

It would be very time-consuming if you had to use the brush to color in every object you create. To make adding color to whole sections of an object faster, the Mental Canvas development team has included a Fill

Tool – the Paint Bucket, ⬛. Once you have your object drawn and you are ready to add color, tap the Paint Bucket icon, choose your color, and tap in the object wherever you want to add that color. ***Note:*** If you should see a paint buck with a red "X" in it, ✎, you have a gap somewhere in the section you are trying to color. Find it, close it, and use the Paint Bucket again (see Figure 3-9).

If you get this when trying to use the Paint Bucket to fill an area, check for gaps.

Figure 3-9. *You cannot fill any areas where gaps exist*

Should you make a mistake at any time while drawing, tap the Eraser

icon, ![eraser icon], to switch to the eraser tool. Use your Apple Pencil to trace over the area you wish to erase. Those readers with pens that have erasers on the end opposite the pen nib can simply turn the pen around and apply the eraser directly to the canvas to begin erasing. Other pens have buttons that must be pressed to activate the eraser. Whichever type of eraser your device supports, the eraser tool is a quick and convenient way to delete any mistakes you make without having to use the selection and editing tools unnecessarily.

And finally, the Mental Canvas team has provided a tool by which you can add color to your designs. While one of the Mental Canvas trainers calls it the Color Picker (Mental Canvas 2021), I have chosen to refer to it as the Color Palette. This is in keeping with the industry standard and not meant to confuse the reader. Either description works.

To access the Color Palette, tap its icon: ![color palette icon]. Figure 3-10 explains the three methods by which the palette may be used to select colors.

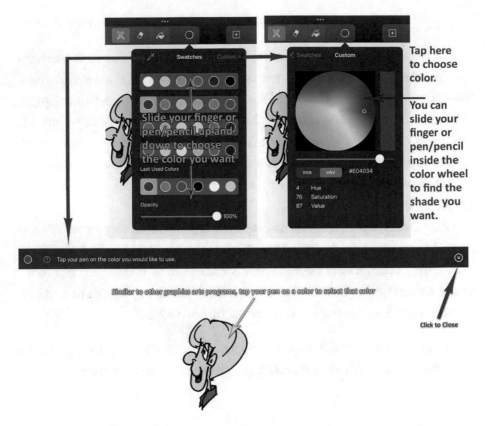

Figure 3-10. *The Color Palette makes it possible to choose color in three ways*

The first method is simply to swipe up and down on the color swatches that first appear when the palette is opened. The Mental Canvas team has provided 48 swatches of colors.

The second method, should the 48 swatches not have the color with which you want to work, is to tap the *Custom* link. This will open a color wheel that you can then tap to select the desired color. You can choose from RGB or HSV color palettes. Use the slider below the wheel to adjust the color range.

To use the third method, tap the Eyedropper icon, , to select the Eyedropper tool. As with other graphics applications, you use the eyedropper to sample the color you wish to use. Once sampled, the palette is filled with that color, and you can then apply it with the Brush or the Paint Bucket tool.

This is useful when the color you wish to use is not one of the default swatch colors and is no longer available in the *Last Used Colors* section of the palette. Simply tap the Eyedropper tool, sample the color you want to use, and continue working.

Summary

In this chapter, we explored the use of the basic drawing tools that included the selection and editing tools, the Brushes Panel, the eraser tool, the paint bucket fill tool, and the color palette. These tools allow readers to express themselves quickly in a format even beginners find easy to follow and simple to use. In the next chapter, we will explore the Parallel Projection tools and learn how they can be used in conjunction with the canvas.

Practical Exercises

Now that you are familiar with the drawing tools, begin experimenting with each of the tools discussed in this chapter.

- Draw a design or image on the main canvas
  - ○ Use the Selection tools to select and edit it
- Play with each of the available brushes
  - ○ Get comfortable using them
  - ○ Select your favorite
- Familiarize yourself with the paint bucket fill tool
- Make mistakes and use the eraser to correct them
- Play with the color palette and get used to all three methods for choosing colors.

Bibliography

Dorsey, Julie, and Sam Nassour. 2021. *Mental Canvas: Drawing Reimagined – Lightbox Expo 2021*. September 13. www.youtube.com/watch?v=QoZe8CHW5jc.

Gallagher, Tyler. 2021. *Meet The Inventors: Julie Dorsey of Mental Canvas On How To Go From Idea To Store Shelf (Question 1)*. September 23. Accessed March 4, 2022. https://medium.com/p/f327105d3922.

Mental Canvas. 2016–2021. *Frequently Asked Questions*. https://mentalcanvas.com/faq.

Mental Canvas. 2016–2021. *Mental Canvas expands drawing and enhances expression*. https://mentalcanvas.com/pro.

Mental Canvas. 2022. *Mental Canvas in the News*. Accessed March 4, 2022. https://mentalcanvas.com/company/press.

Mental Canvas. 2021. *Selection and Editing Tools.* October 4. `https://youtu.be/b9b5mZ8Ff7A`.

Mental Canvas Support. January 13, 2022. *Personal communication via email.*

Mental Canvas. 2016–2021. *The Mental Canvas Story.* `https://mentalcanvas.com/about`.

In His Own Words – Greg Edwards

Background

I'm an artist living in Belfast, Northern Ireland, with a background in architecture, architectural visualization and art direction. Over the last year or so I've found myself working mostly in the sporting world, which includes producing artwork for the NFL, PGA, and Fox, to name a few. I balance my time between working on commissioned projects and my own personal work which is largely fine art based. I'm highly interested in collaborations, immersive storytelling, fantasy art, and oil painting.

Mental Canvas Journey

My Mental Canvas journey started in mid-2021 when they held a competition to share art made on MC online. An absolutely brilliant idea as it resulted in tens of millions of views from various artists' submissions and really helped them grow on social media. I immediately clicked with Mental Canvas as a software as it allowed me to apply my understanding of more traditional drawing techniques and apply to this new medium. I became interested in immersive storytelling, where the user would be encouraged to explore the artwork through a series of revealing layers.

I was fortunate enough that my work went viral across platforms towards the end of 2021, which would never have been possible had it not been for Mental Canvas's persistence in wanting to share my work on their social channels. They reached out a few times and finally one evening, having just left the office quite late, I decided to head back up and turn my computer on to upload the mental canvas scene to their servers.

The next morning I woke up to thousands of followers and an uncountable number of likes on my Instagram. I had no clue at first where it was coming from however quickly traced it back to Mental Canvases Tiktok where their post of my work was getting several hundred thousand views.

To cut a long story short, my work started making its way across various social media platforms but it was Linkedin and consequently the NFL that reached out via that network to propose a collaboration for the Superbowl. So had Mental Canvas never reached out, I'd never had got those major commissions which has since sculpted my career as an independent artist.

Why I Chose Mental Canvas and Thoughts on Application

As I've already mentioned, I discovered Mental Canvas because of their competition but I've continued to use it as I find it a great storytelling tool. I love the effect of revealing more artwork as you interactively explore the scene as it allows users to engage with the artwork in a previously impossible way.

What I also like about Mental Canvas is its ability to collaborate with other drawing tools. Whilst I do frequently use Mental Canvas for personal projects where I can just go with the flow and sketch in the 2.5D space using their inbuilt brush sets, the ability to import JPEGS or PNGS adds an extra layer of robustness for more serious things like commissions. This is a significant and important feature as it allows for continued interactive design which is prevalent in a commercial environment. My tool of choice for digital painting is Procreate, which is also available on the Ipad, so combined with Mental Canvas you've got a arsenal of tools that allow you to make serious artwork on the go.

Overall I think Mental Canvas is a brilliant tool that's easy to use for artists of any skill range and I'll continue to use it as part of my pipeline.

Kind regards,

Greg
Belfast, Northern Ireland

CHAPTER 4

The Canvas

Assuming you have been following along on your touch device, you now have a working knowledge of the Mental Canvas application. You have been able to download and install the application, license it, and create your first scene. You have begun using the drawing and editing tools and you are thinking to yourself, "That's it? I don't see the difference between this and any other drawing app." And that is where what you will learn in this and subsequent chapters enters the picture (pun intended). Here are this chapter's objectives.

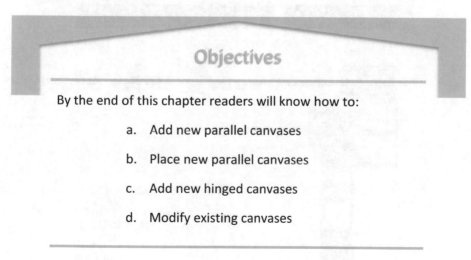

Objectives

By the end of this chapter readers will know how to:

a. Add new parallel canvases

b. Place new parallel canvases

c. Add new hinged canvases

d. Modify existing canvases

M. Commini, *Mental Canvas for Training and Development*,
https://doi.org/10.1007/978-1-4842-8774-3_4

The Canvas

As mentioned earlier, Mental Canvas gives you the power to create depth and animated fly-through effects that allow your 2D presentations to come alive! Using the tools and techniques in these next chapters gives you the power to create *virtual* 3D scenes that draw your audience into your presentations, where they can explore, gather information, and *learn* in a fun and entertaining way – rather than sit on the sidelines viewing static images, trying to stay awake as the after-lunch sugar slump hits.

Adding Depth to Your 2D Image

Recall from the overview that there are two panels that, by default, exist on the canvas in the top left corner. They are the Canvas Panel and the Layers Panel (see Figure 4-1).

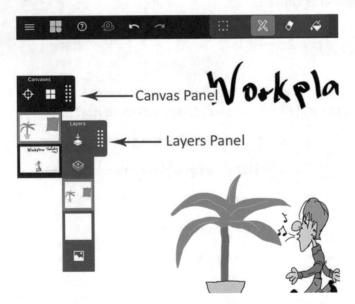

Figure 4-1. *The Canvas and Layers Panels are located by default in the top left*

Floating above all canvases, they exist in three states: fully closed, partially extended, and fully extended (see Figure 4-2).

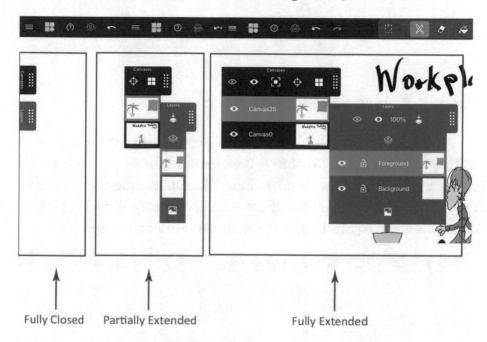

Fully Closed   Partially Extended   Fully Extended

Figure 4-2. *Three states of existence*

As previously stated, scenes are composed of canvases, and canvases are composed of layers. Canvases allow you to create depth in your Mental Canvas scene, and layers allow you to organize the content you place on each canvas. Without the ability to add new canvases, your scenes would remain static two-dimensional images, and you would not achieve the spatial effects Mental Canvas is known for.

Adding New Canvases

To add a new parallel canvas, select either *Drawing* or *Viewing Mode* and click on the *Add New Canvas* tool icon (Figure 4-3). For the following examples, *Drawing Mode* was used unless indicated otherwise.

Figure 4-3. *Adding a new canvas to your scene*

A new parallel canvas is created in front of your existing canvas. You will immediately notice two things. First, the new canvas is completely transparent and is represented by a blue field. And second, it is parallel to the existing canvas. Figure 4-4 shows the new canvas from the landscape orientation, and Figure 4-5 shows it from the portrait orientation.

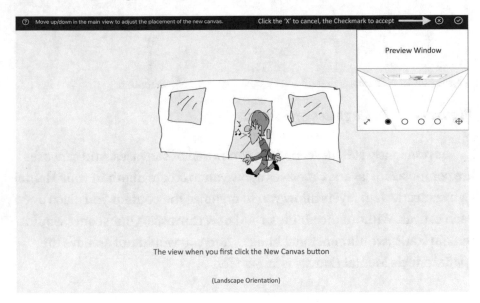

Figure 4-4. *Landscape orientation of a new canvas*

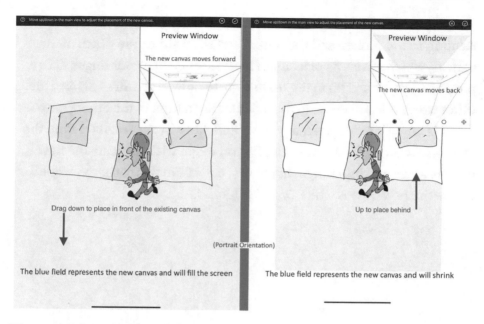

Figure 4-5. *Portrait orientation of a new canvas*

As you can see from both figures, a *Preview Window*[1] also appears in the top right corner of the canvas. Since the canvas is transparent, this window allows you to see the canvas' placement while you adjust its depth relative to your other canvases. By tapping on one of the four buttons, you can change the viewpoint relative to the camera (see Figure 4-6).

The four viewpoints are top down, with the camera situated in the bottom of the window; from the side, with the camera situated to the left; diagonally with the camera situated in the bottom left corner; and from the front, with the camera situated directly in front of you. Please note: The *Preview Window* shows the canvas' position in relation to the camera position in the *Preview Window*. The main view is always viewed from whichever direction it was facing when you tapped the *New Canvas* button (see Figure 4-7).

---

[1] Note that at least one Mental Canvas trainer refers to the Preview Window as a Bird's Eye View. Using either designation is correct.

These different viewpoints allow you to see the canvas placement in relation to the camera and the other canvas. To adjust the depth of the canvas, which affects its placement in the scene, drag your finger, active pen, or Apple Pencil up in the main view to move the canvas behind the other canvases, and down to move it further in front of the other canvases.

It is important to note that you should place the new canvas from the view you wish to affect. For example, you might wish to create the new canvas while looking straight at the first canvas. In this case, you would create the new canvas while *Drawing Mode* is on.

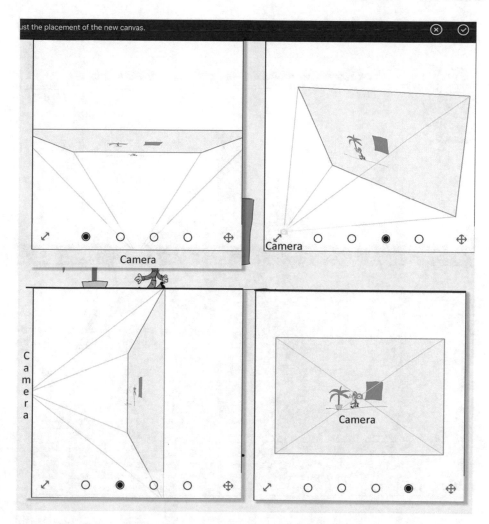

Figure 4-6. Preview Window views relative to the camera

On the other hand, while in *Viewing Mode,* you might wish to rotate your existing canvas and create your new canvas from a side view. Your new canvas will always be created from whichever view you begin with (see Figure 4-7). This will be explored further when we cover the Bookmarks Panel and creating the fly-through animations.

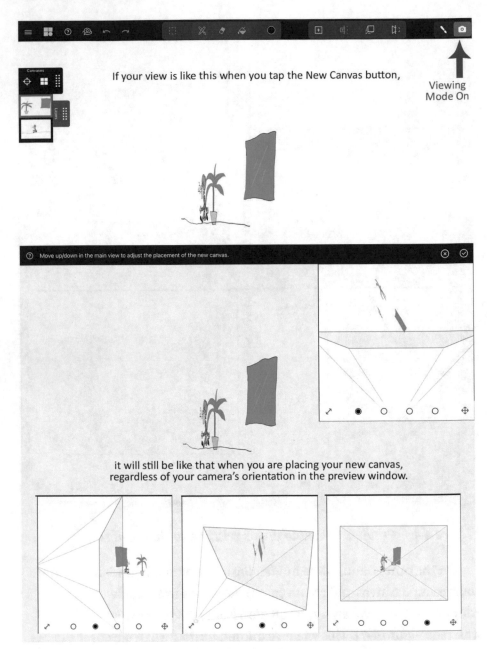

Figure 4-7. *The main view is always as it was when you created the new canvas*

Figure 4-8 shows the new canvas when placed straight on in *Drawing Mode*, while Figure 4-9 shows the effect you can achieve with *Viewing Mode* on. Notice that you can barely see the third canvas when in *Drawing Mode*. This is because I created it while the first two canvases were rotated approximately 45 degrees to the left while in *Viewing Mode*. In this way, I was able to create a "wall" that can only be seen when rotating the canvas in that mode.

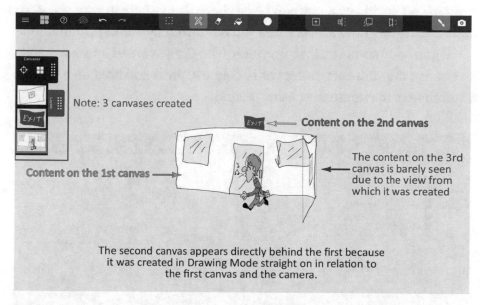

Figure 4-8. *Canvas placement depends on the point of view when created*

Figure 4-9 might be a little misleading. As can be seen by the icons in the top right of the workspace, the screenshot was taken in *Drawing Mode*, yet the content of the third canvas is clearly in view. This is because its canvas was the selected canvas on the *Canvas Panel*. Notice the blue lines around the top icon of the *Canvas Panel*? Those blue lines tell you which canvas is currently selected and ready to work with. The view automatically defaults to position the content of the selected canvas in front of you. In this way, you can place content anywhere in your scene and create some very cool effects when you build your fly-through animation.

Figure 4-10 shows a close-up view of the *Canvas Panel* fully extended. To change the name of a canvas or to delete it, press and hold on it to open a submenu and choose the desired action.

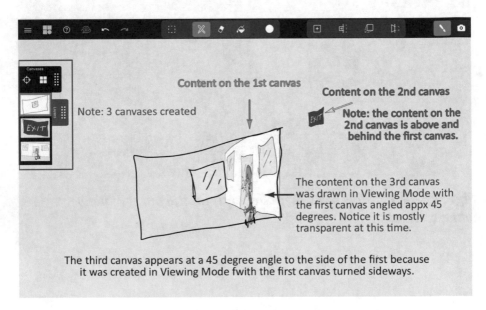

Figure 4-9. *The third canvas was created in Viewing Mode*

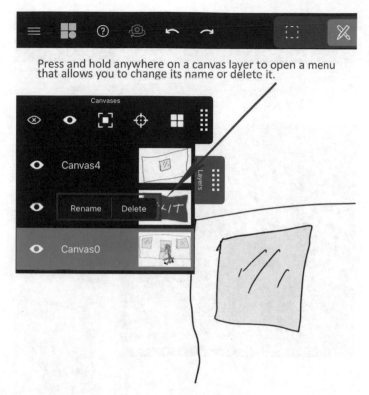

Figure 4-10. *The Canvas Panel fully extended*

To hide a canvas, tap the eye icon, , to the left of the canvas' name (see Figure 4-11). Hiding canvases is useful when you have a lot of content on multiple canvases and you wish to work in a less distracting environment.

Click on the Eye Icon to hide a canvas

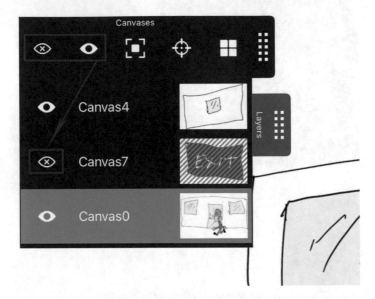

Figure 4-11. *Hiding a canvas is simple*

Figure 4-12 shows the result of tapping the Zoom icon, . This allows you to quickly zoom in on the selected canvas. Suppose, for example, that you discovered you have a hole somewhere in the content of that canvas that is preventing you from using the paint bucket to add fill to an area. Tapping the square icon zooms you in quickly without the need to put your pencil down. You can tap with your finger or you can tap with your pencil. The effect is immediate.

To return to "normal" size, you will need to pinch the canvas with two fingers and squeeze them together.

Figure 4-12. *Fast zoom*

The icon that looks like the target from a periscope, , allows you to quickly select a canvas to work on from multiple canvases. This is especially useful when you have many canvases, your scene is filled with a lot of content, and you are not sure which canvas holds the content with which you want to work.

Touch the icon; drag your pencil over the screen until the canvas you want has been selected. The effect is immediate. Should the wrong canvas be selected because of a cluttered scene, simply repeat the process. Please see Figure 4-13 for an example.

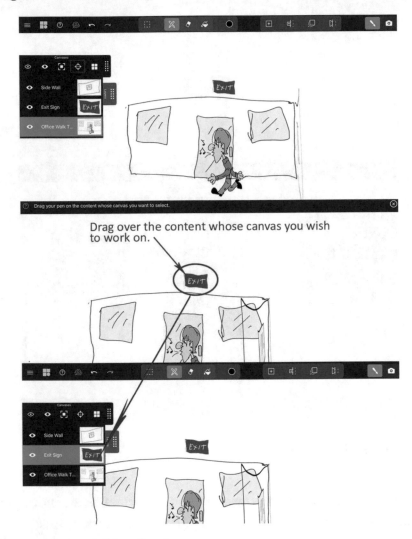

Figure 4-13. *Quickly selecting a canvas*

And finally, the icon that looks like a windowpane, ⊞ , "is a handy way to focus on the canvas you're working on. This will reduce the opacity of all other canvases in your scene to make them appear faded, so that it's easier to see the content on the canvas you're working on (without needing to actually hide the other canvases)".[2]

Adding Hinges

Recall from Figures 4-7, 4-8, and 4-9 that I used *Viewing Mode* to place a canvas at an angle to the other canvases. While I drew the content of the canvas in *Viewing Mode* by physically rotating the canvases in the scene prior to creating the new canvas, I could have easily added the new canvas in *Drawing Mode* without the need to rotate the other canvases.

I could have done this using another of the Projection tools – the Add Hinged Canvas tool – ⊞ ◧ ▢ ▢ . Adding hinges in your designs allows you to intersect your existing canvases with new angled canvases that hinge around an axis point you choose.

To set it, drag the two outer handles to your chosen point. Figure 4-14 shows an example of setting the axis point.

---

[2] R. Resnic, 2022. Personal communication, March 9.

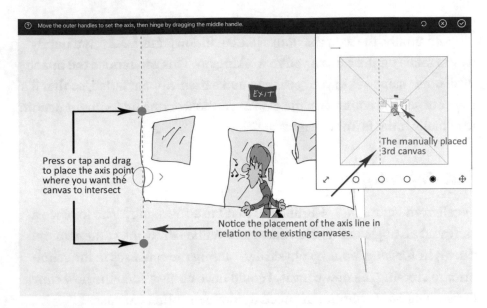

Figure 4-14. *Setting the axis point for a new, hinged canvas*

Once your axis point has been set, drag the center handle to create the angle of the new canvas. You can drag the handle in any direction until you achieve the result you wish to use.

In the top image of Figure 4-15, you can see the placement of the new hinged canvas in relation to the existing canvas in the *Preview Window*. Tapping the check mark to accept this placement closes the window and returns you to the main view. The bottom image of Figure 4-15 now shows a fourth canvas has been created in the *Canvas Panel*. Notice we achieved in the *Drawing Mode* the same effect using the *New Hinged Canvas* tool that we achieved placing the third canvas manually in the *Viewing Mode*.

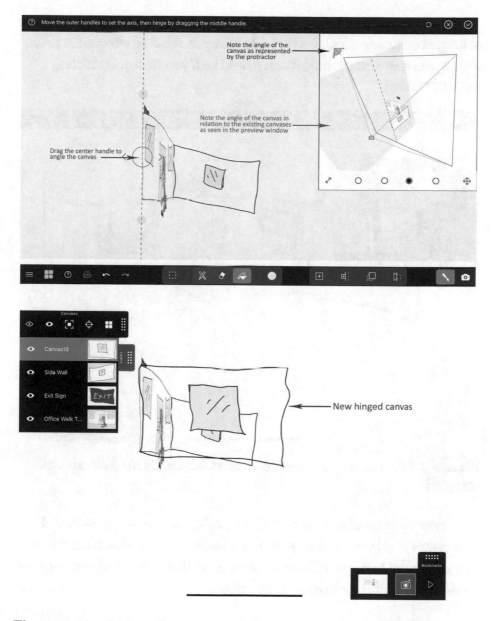

Figure 4-15. *Setting the axis point and angle with the New Hinged Canvas tool*

Figure 4-16 shows the result with the first canvas selected. Creative use of hinged canvases allows you to build many interesting effects that make your scene more interesting than it would be if you were just creating a static 2D image.

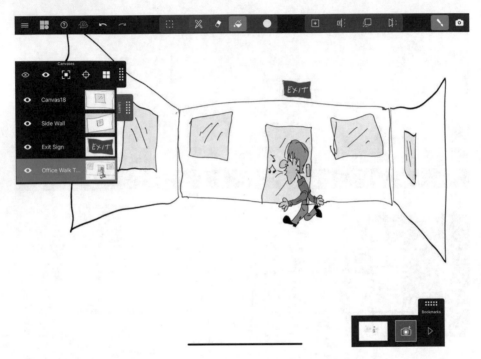

Figure 4-16. *The new hinged canvas as seen with the first canvas selected*

Some of those effects include adding bridges, skyways, streets, and causeways to interactive maps, building walls that your viewers can rotate or pan around to reveal hidden content, and adding different perspectives while maintaining the original scene view.

Working with Existing Canvases

Up to now, we have been working with new canvases: adding, placing, modifying. But what do you do if you decide to make placement changes to existing parallel canvases? What options do you have if you decide to change the perspective of an existing canvas? Fortunately, the Mental Canvas developers considered those possibilities and gave us the tools needed to make those changes.

Notice the last two icons in the suite of *Parallel Projection* tools do not have plus signs – ▢ ▢ ▢ ▢ . They are from left to right, the *Parallel Projection* tool and the *Hinged Canvas* tool.

The Parallel Projection tool, ▢ , allows you to adjust the placement of your parallel canvases in the same way you did when you created them – pull the canvas down to move it in front of the existing canvases and push it up to move it behind the existing canvases (see Figure 4-17).

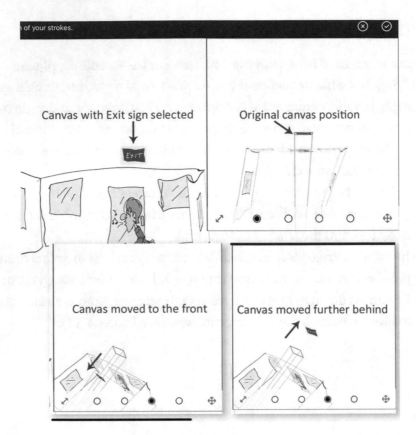

Figure 4-17. *Using the Parallel Projection tool*

And finally, the Hinged Canvas tool, ⊡ , allows you to take an existing canvas and change its angle relative to the other existing canvases. As you would when placing a *New Hinged Canvas*, use the outer handles to set your axis point around which the canvas will rotate and then drag the middle handle to create the hinge for your canvas (see Figure 4-18).

Hinged canvases are useful for changing the perspective of the content of the canvas in relation to the other parallel canvases. For example, if your design team is creating an office safety training, they could draw representations of the office layouts, including any open office plans, on parallel canvases and then use the Hinge tool to accurately reposition each office and cubicle in relation to your company's main area.

Then when the employees view the interactive presentation on the company's LMS, they would be able to pan and fly through the presentation identifying safety hazards throughout the building. Later in the book we will explore adding photos to your Mental Canvas presentation so you could use actual images instead of artists' renderings.

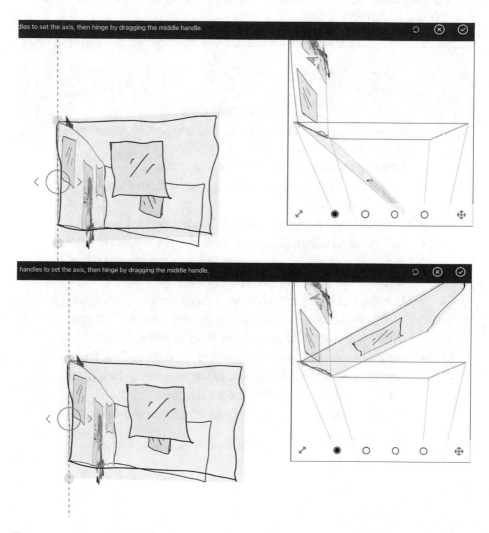

Figure 4-18. *Using the hinge tool to adjust existing canvases*

Summary

In this chapter, we explored the *Canvas Panel* and learned how to create new parallel and hinged canvases and how to adjust their positioning in relation to existing canvases. We did this using the *New Canvas* and *New Hinged Canvas* tools, found in the *Parallel Projection* tool suite. We also learned how to adjust existing canvases using the *Parallel Projection* and *Hinged Canvas* tools. In the next chapter, we will explore the *Layers Panel*.

Practical Exercises

- Open an existing scene or create a new one.
- Locate the Canvas Panel on the left hand side of your device's screen.
- If it is open, tap it to minimize it. Tap it again to close it.
- Use the *New Canvas* tool in the *Parallel Projection* tool suite to create a new canvas. Use the Preview Window to adjust its position relative to the other parallel canvases.
- Use the *New Hinged Canvas* tool in the *Parallel Projection* tool suite to create a new hinged canvas. Use the Preview Window to adjust its position relative to the other canvases.
- Long press one of the thumbnails in the *Canvas Panel* to open the sub-menu and select either *Rename* or *Delete* to rename or delete the canvas accordingly.
- Familiarize yourself with the tools across the top of the canvas panel.

SECTION III

Layers, Bookmarks, and Beyond

Note: From this point forward, you may wish to utilize the files provided by me and by Apress. Please do the following:

Retrieve the files from GitHub. They are located here: `https://github.com/Apress/Mental-Canvas-for-Training-and-Development`.

On Windows Devices: Download the files into whichever location on your Windows device works best for your workflow.

On the iPad Pro: Use the files app to navigate to the root files location on your iPad Pro and open the Mental Canvas folder. Place all files ending in .mcs into this folder.

Next, create a Mental Canvas album in your Photos app and place all the image files into this album. The limitations of iOS make it necessary to place the images into the photo album to be able to use Mental Canvas' image import feature.

See Figure P3-1 for a visual representation of what you might see using the Split View feature.

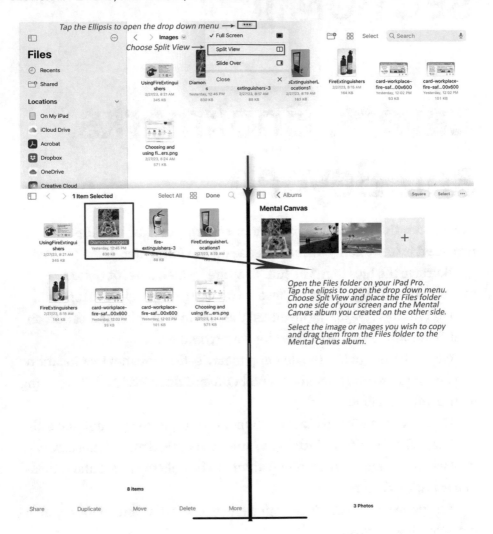

Figure P3-1. *Using Split View on the iPad Pro*

CHAPTER 5

Layers and Importing Images

In the previous chapters, we explored choosing the right Mental Canvas plan for you and your team, the systems compatible with the application, downloading and installing the application, creating your first scene and the file management associated with it, the two main views available with which to create your projects, and adding, editing, and manipulating canvases to add depth to your scenes.

In this chapter, we will examine the foundations of those canvases and learn how to keep content organized for the most efficient presentation for your learners.

Here are this chapter's objectives.

© Michael Commini 2023
M. Commini, *Mental Canvas for Training and Development*,
https://doi.org/10.1007/978-1-4842-8774-3_5

Objectives

By the end of this chapter readers will know how to:

a. Add new layers

b. Edit and manipulate layers

c. Import images

d. Use the selection tools to manipulate images

e. Import Layers from external apps

Working with Layers

As you can see in Figure 5-1, when you create a canvas, you create two layers for that canvas in the *Layers Panel*. One layer is the background layer, and the other is the foreground layer. By tapping and holding on the layer name, you can call up a submenu that allows you to either rename the layer or delete it. You can also reposition a layer by pressing and holding the layer and then dragging it into a new position.

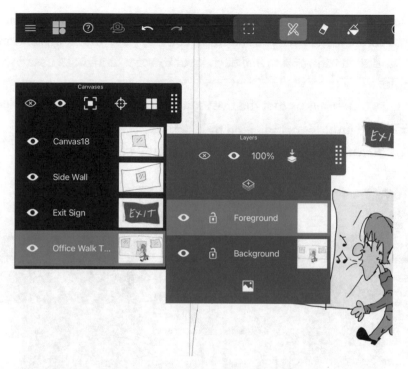

Figure 5-1. *Every canvas starts with two layers*

If you are familiar with Adobe® Photoshop®, the GNU Image Manipulation Program (GIMP), Corel® PaintShop® Pro, or other graphics software,[1] you are already familiar with using layers to organize your creatives. Mental Canvas offers a basic layer feature similar to those software applications. We will explore those features now.

As with the *Canvas Panel*, the *Layers Panel* exists in three states:[2] completely closed, partially extended (thumbnail view), and fully extended. To close or extend the *Layers Panel*, tap the double row of dots in the upper right corner of the panel. Tap the *Eye* icon to the left of the

---

[1] Adobe and Photoshop are registered trademarks of Adobe Inc.; Corel and PaintShop Pro are registered trademarks of Corel Corporation.

[2] The Mental Canvas trainer says there are two "states." Apparently "completely closed" is not considered a "state" to the Mental Canvas team. They are wrong.

Lock icon to hide or reveal the layer. Hiding a layer is useful when you want to try different ideas with your content. You can put content on separate layers and then hide and reveal each layer to see which looks best, for example.

Figure 5-2 shows us that the Eye icon has two states: hidden, indicated by 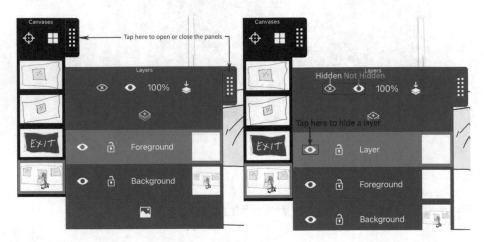, and unhidden, indicated by ██.

To add a new layer, tap the *New Layer* icon (see Figure 5-3).

Figure 5-2. *Extending the Layers Panel and hiding layers*

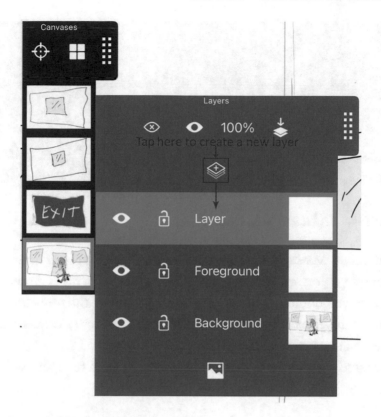

Figure 5-3. *Adding a new layer*

To adjust the opacity of a layer, tap on 100% to the right of the *Eye* icon. This will open a slider bar with which you adjust the layer's opacity. How transparent the layer becomes is indicated as a percentage and changes as you move the slider in either direction until you get to 0, completely transparent, or 100%, completely opaque (see Figure 5-4). Adjusting the opacity of a layer is useful when you wish to trace an element or object on the layer below or when you want

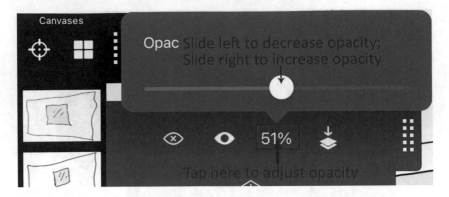

Figure 5-4. *Adjusting layer opacity*

content on one layer to "bleed through" to content on another layer. For example, if you are working on a storybook that involves monsters and ghosts, you could put the ghosts on a layer above the monsters and then adjust the ghost layer opacity until the ghosts are translucent and the monsters can be "seen" through them.

To merge layers, tap the *Merge Layer* icon, as seen in Figure 5-5.

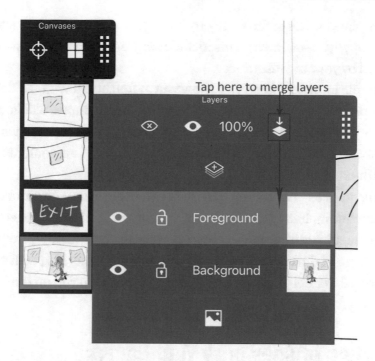

Figure 5-5. *Merging layers*

Importing Images into Your Project

In this chapter, we will work with imported images. Therefore, it is important to note that to protect your organization from lawsuits for violating someone's intellectual property rights, your creative team *must* respect the copyright laws of your country and, in the case where any content you purchase or download for use was produced by a source outside your country, the copyright laws of the country of origin.

Copyright[3] exists to protect the rights to own and distribute original works made by creatives. In the United States, copyright is instant as soon

---

[3] I am not an attorney. It is important you contact a knowledgeable intellectual property attorney to be sure you remain firmly within the law.

as the original author of the work produces it, whether or not the work bears a copyright statement. This includes any original creative work produced by your organization.

A simple Internet search will allow you to find and download content for your projects from many sources. Some of those sources will be public domain – content for which the copyright has expired, or which has been placed into the public domain by the content creator. This content may be used without attribution to the original author/creator.

Other sources[4] may require payment of a license fee with strict use requirements, including attribution of the creator. And still other sources may only require attribution – recognition somewhere within your project of the creator of the content you have chosen to use. Working with a knowledgeable intellectual property attorney will keep you on the "straight and narrow."

Importing Images onto Your Layers

While Mental Canvas is a great application with various brushes and colors for use by you and your team for free hand drawing, it would be a poor application if it did not also provide the ability to bring images into your project from external sources. This provides you and your team of creatives the ability to use applications such as Adobe Photoshop®, GIMP®, Adobe Illustrator®, Adobe Fresco®, Procreate®, and other drawing, painting, and sketching applications that produce images in either the .jpg or .png format.[5]

---

[4] Unless otherwise noted, all images and drawings in this chapter were created and/or produced by me.

[5] As mentioned elsewhere, Adobe, Adobe Photoshop, Adobe Illustrator, and Adobe Fresco are registered trademarks of Adobe Inc. Procreate® is a registered trademark of Savage Interactive Pty Ltd. GIMP is open source and not trademarked.

The Mental Canvas team made it very easy to import images from outside the Mental Canvas application. Simply by tapping on the picture icon at the bottom of the *Layers Panel,* you can bring images onto their own layers (Figure 5-6). Try it now.

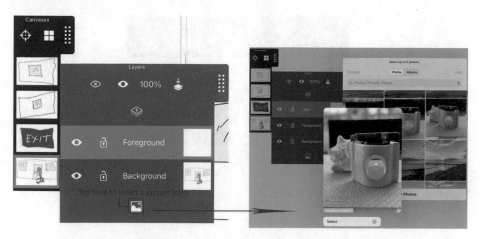

Figure 5-6. *Importing an image onto a layer*

1. (Refer to Figure 5-8 if you would prefer a visual example.) Click on the hamburger menu to open the drop-down menu.

2. Locate the Mental Canvas root folder on your device and double-click it to open it.

3. Double-click on the Chapter Five Files folder to open it.

4. Locate and double-click on the Ch5WorkingWithImages.mcs file to open the scene.

You will notice the scene was created using the Foreground Midground Background template included with Mental Canvas. Should your scene open in the Viewing Mode, click on the brush to switch to the Drawing Mode. This will orient you so you are facing the canvas (see Figure 5-7).

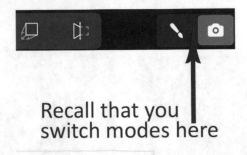

Recall that you
switch modes here

Figure 5-7. *Switching modes*

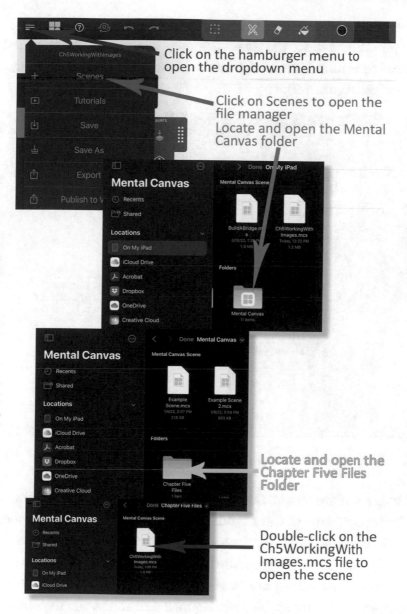

Click on the hamburger menu to open the dropdown menu

Click on Scenes to open the file manager
Locate and open the Mental Canvas folder

Locate and open the Chapter Five Files Folder

Double-click on the Ch5WorkingWith Images.mcs file to open the scene

Figure 5-8. *Opening a scene*

Next, extend the Canvas Palette to see the canvases and extend the Layers Palette to see the layers. Choose a canvas and its associated unlocked foreground layer. Click on the image icon to open the image browser (see Figure 5-9).

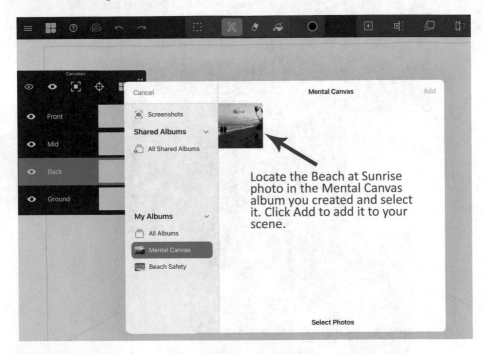

Figure 5-9. *Selecting an image for import*

Navigate to the Mental Canvas album you created and select the *Beach at Sunrise* image. Click "Add" to import the image into your scene. Figure 5-10 shows you the options you have to resize and rotate the image. Figure 5-11A shows you the resolution options with which you can import your images. They are 2K and Full Resolution. Using the 2K option generates smaller project file sizes. Figure 5-11B shows you the options to cancel (reject) or accept the image importation. Simply tap with your pencil/pen on the "X" to reject the importation and tap with your pencil/pen on the check mark to accept the image importation.

Importing images at full resolution may lead to performance issues. Figure 5-12 is an example of the warning message you might receive. You can continue importing at the higher resolution, but your system might slow down or encounter other unexpected issues. Click "Close" to acknowledge the message. Of course, you also have the option of rejecting the image and using an image editing application such as Adobe Photoshop or GIMP to change the resolution, re-save the file, and try your import again. That is the joy of being a creative ... the satisfaction we get at the end of the day for a project well done based on *our* choices!

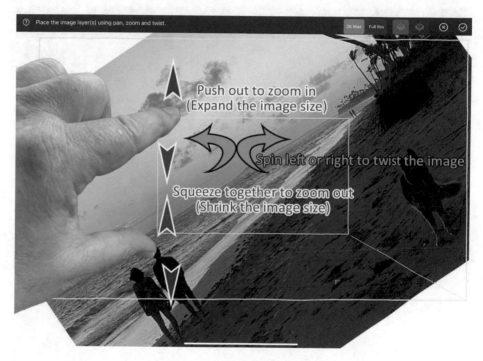

Figure 5-10. *Resizing and rotating your image*

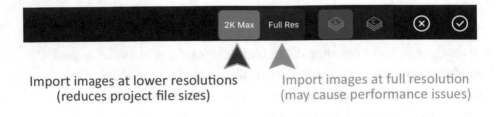

2K Max
Full Res
Import images at lower resolutions (reduces project file sizes)
Import images at full resolution (may cause performance issues)

Figure 5-11A

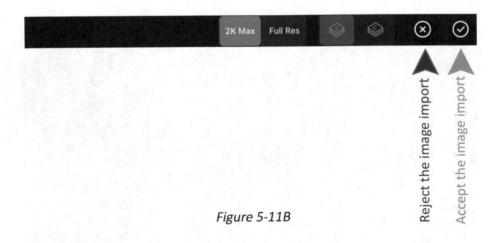

2K Max
Full Res
Reject the image import
Accept the image import

Figure 5-11B

Figure 5-11. *Image resolution and accepting/rejecting the image*

Figure 5-12. *Warning message when importing images at full resolution*

Beginning with Figure 5-13, the following images walk you step-by-step through the process of creating a new scene and selecting one of the templates provided by the Mental Canvas team for your convenience.

As mentioned in a previous chapter, the Mental Canvas team has provided templates for your use. Each template represents a scene made up of specific canvases. For this chapter, I have chosen the Foreground Midground Background template. This template provides several options that will demonstrate some of the available features.

You can see from Figure 5-13 that the template, which represents your scene, contains multiple canvases. They are (1) the front canvas, (2) the midground canvas, (3) the background canvas, and (4) the ground canvas. I have highlighted each to make it easier to see the distinction.

It is important to remember to select which canvas you want to work on from the canvas palette. This puts that canvas in the front, or head-on, camera view. This is important to keep your content in the proper view and perspective. Figure 5-14A and 5-14B provides a visual explanation of what I mean.

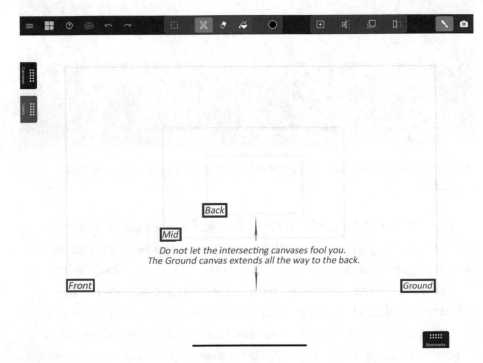

Figure 5-13. *The multiple canvases provided with the FMB template*

In Figure 5-14A, I positioned the ground canvas in the front camera view and placed a sunrise image taken at the beach outside my home in the Caribbean on the associated layer. Notice the image appears full on, as it should since you are looking at it straight on. Also notice the template guides. They represent each of the canvases. You can see that the image extends past the ground canvas guides toward the Back canvas. You can also see that the image does not fit the ground canvas' perspective as it is drawn. This is not a problem as you can hide the layer with the guides in the finished presentation.

In Figure 5-14B, the front canvas is in the front camera position. This has rotated the ground canvas into the ground position. Notice the difference? The ground does not look quite right now, with the sunrise lying flat. By changing your camera view frequently while creating your content, you can assure you have everything placed correctly. This enhances what your viewer will experience with your finished presentation.

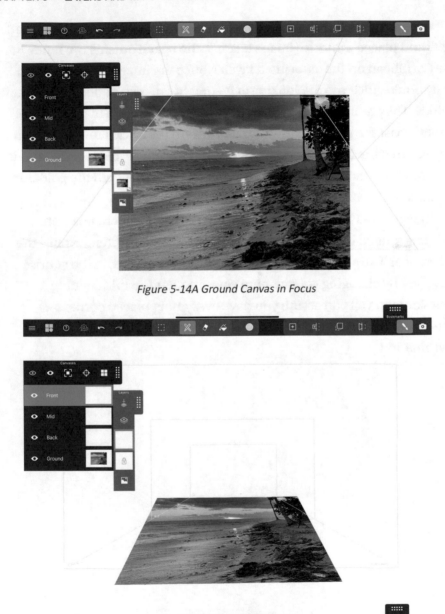

Figure 5-14A Ground Canvas in Focus

Figure 5-14B Front Canvas in Focus

Figure 5-14. *Keep your canvas in the Front View to accurately place content*

To further assist you in visualizing the canvas placements for this template, I provide Figure 5-15. Figure 5-15A shows the front canvas straight on and the effect this has on the ground canvas. Notice that you can barely see the ground canvas.

Figure 5-15B demonstrates the relationship between the two canvases once they have been set in place. Notice the ground canvas is on a different plane.

Figure 5-15A The Front canvas content appears above the Ground canvas content

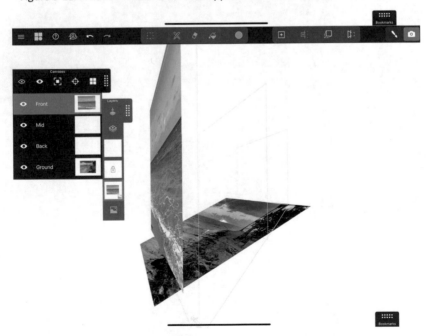

Figure 5-15B In reality, the Ground canvas is on a different plane

Figure 5-15. *The ground and front canvases relative to each other*

We will explore how to resize your images once you have set them in place a little later in this chapter. You can use the template guides to set your images where you want them and resize them as needed. Once everything is to your satisfaction, tap the (check mark) to set the image in place and return to the canvas view. As previously mentioned, if you change your mind, tap the (X) to cancel the import.

Editing Images

There may come a time when you wish to edit your images, such as duplicating, removing, or moving selected areas of your imported images to a new canvas. Mental Canvas comes with some basic image editing tools, which we will cover now. For more heavy-duty requirements, a more robust image editing program should be used.

Remember Harvey Rumplemeyer from Chapters 1 and 2? Figure 5-16 shows Harvey as he stands next to his space-time machine. The image is a flat .png file. In this case, I chose to use a .png file rather than a .jpg because .png files support transparent backgrounds while .jpg files do not. This is important when wanting to edit portions of your image without having to compensate for any background colors. In this case, I painted the background white for the snow when I drew the image for my book. So I still need to remove the white when I edit the image.

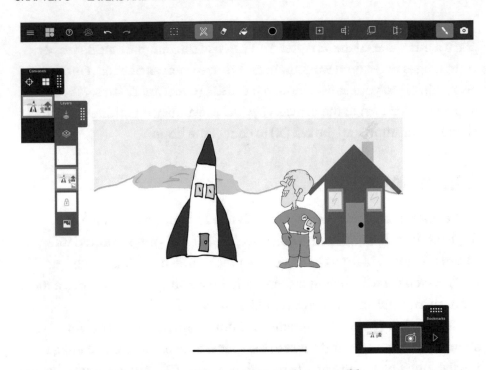

Figure 5-16. *Harvey Rumplemeyer in a flat .png file*

The top image in Figure 5-17 shows an example of the same .png file with the white-colored (the snow, ice, and sky) background enabled. The bottom image shows it with the background layer hidden. The result is a transparent background when the file is saved as a .png.

Figure 5-17. *Harvey Rumplemeyer in a flat .png file*

Saving images with transparent backgrounds allows you to select individual items more easily in your image when editing. We will see an example of that in the Project – Fire Safety chapter. For now, we will explore how to select individual items and do what Mental Canvas does best – take a flat two-dimensional image and create a three-dimensional effect!

Recall from Chapter 3 using the Brush and Lasso tools to select and deselect portions of your drawings on a canvas. Editing imported images is similar with a slight difference: using the Brush tool will select the whole image rather than just a part of it. Figure 5-18 shows you an example of using the Brush tool to select from an imported image.

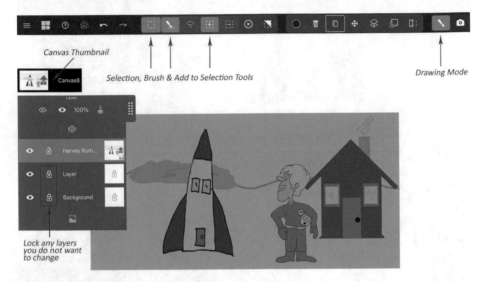

Figure 5-18. *Using the Brush tool to select the entire imported image*

To select just a part of an imported image, you must use the Lasso tool and its associated "Add To" or "Subtract From" the selection buttons (the Mental Canvas team calls them "toggles"). If you look carefully at Figure 5-19A, you will see a blue line surrounding a beautiful King Shepherd dog enjoying the morning sunrise. This is Diamond. That blue line surrounding Diamond is drawn when using the Lasso tool. It indicates the area of the imported image that is being selected.

Figure 5-19B shows that part of Diamond that was selected once the blue line was closed by both ends meeting. Once selected, I could have manipulated the selection by moving it to another area of the layer, projecting it to another canvas, moving it to another layer on the same canvas, deleting it, inverting the selection, or hinging the selection.

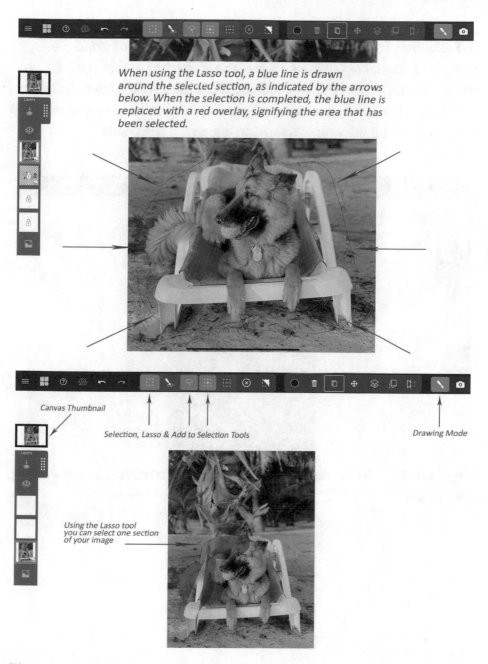

When using the Lasso tool, a blue line is drawn around the selected section, as indicated by the arrows below. When the selection is completed, the blue line is replaced with a red overlay, signifying the area that has been selected.

Canvas Thumbnail

Selection, Lasso & Add to Selection Tools

Drawing Mode

Using the Lasso tool you can select one section of your image

Figure 5-19. *Use the Lasso tool to select part of an image*

Figure 5-20 is the same image with Diamond fully selected. To make the selection, I could have carefully traced around Diamond and the lounger to minimize selecting parts of the overall image that I did not want. Instead, I used the Lasso tool to make a broader selection. Once selected, I switched to the *Subtract From* the selection button and removed the sections I did not want. Figure 5-21 shows the end result.

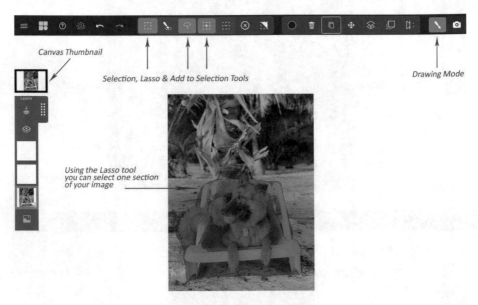

Canvas Thumbnail

Selection, Lasso & Add to Selection Tools

Drawing Mode

Using the Lasso tool you can select one section of your image

Figure 5-20. *The Lasso tool can also be used to select a larger part of an image*

Canvas Thumbnail

Selection, Lasso & Subtract from Selection Tools

Drawing Mode

Compare to the previous image
to see the effect of using the
lasso tool to remove sections
of the image

Figure 5-21. *To remove unwanted areas in your selection, tap the
Subtract From Selection button and use the Lasso tool to highlight the
areas you want removed*

Figures 5-22 and 5-23 provide examples of the effect the various
selection tools have on your image when used for editing. And Figures 5-24
and 5-25 explore the use of the Duplication tool more in depth.

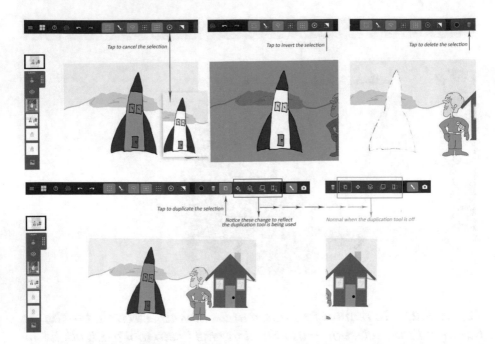

Figure 5-22. *Using the various tools to affect your selection*

Figure 5-22 is a visual example of

- Canceling a selection

- Inverting a selection

- Deleting a selection

- Duplicating a selection

And Figure 5-23 provides a visual example of

- Using the Transform tool

- The New Layer tool

- The Projection tool

- The Hinge Projection tool

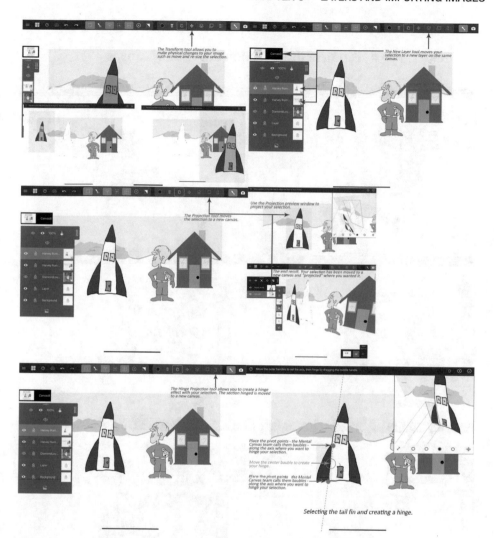

Figure 5-23. *Using the various tools to affect your selection*

Figures 5-24, 5-25, and 5-26 provide visual examples of the available Duplication tool options:

- Transform the selection

- Duplicate the selection onto a new layer

- Duplicate and project the selection onto a new canvas

- Hinge a section of the selection onto a new canvas

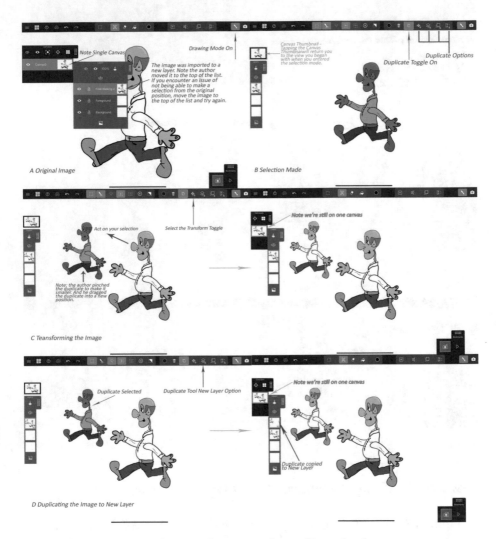

Figure 5-24. *Using the Duplicate tool to edit a single canvas*

Notice that in the original portion of Figure 5-24A, I began with the original image, entered *Selection Mode*, and used the Lasso tool to select it. In Figure 5-24B, I enabled the *Duplicate Tool toggle*. I then selected the *Transform option* (Figure 5-24C) and dragged the selection up and away from the original image and pinched the duplicate to make it smaller. Note that all effects have been performed on one canvas.

In Figure 5-24D, I enabled the *New Layer* toggle, which then copied the selected duplicate to a new layer on the same canvas.

Figure 5-25 is a visual example of using the Duplicate Tool with the Projection option. In Figure 5-25A, I imported the image of Fred to a new layer. You will meet Fred again in the project on Office Fire Safety.

In Figure 5-25B, I enabled Selection Mode and used the brush to select all of Fred. After Fred was selected, I enabled the Duplication tool and selected the Projection option.

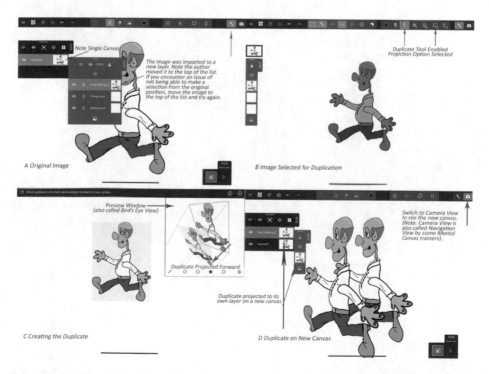

Figure 5-25. *Using the Duplicate tool to project the duplicate to a new canvas*

For Figure 5-25C, I used the Bird's Eye View Preview Window to project the canvas to its own layer on a new Canvas. Figure 5-25D shows a visual example of the finished result.

Figure 5-26 provides a visual walk-through of using the Hinge Projection option with the Duplicate tool to create a hinged projection on a new canvas.

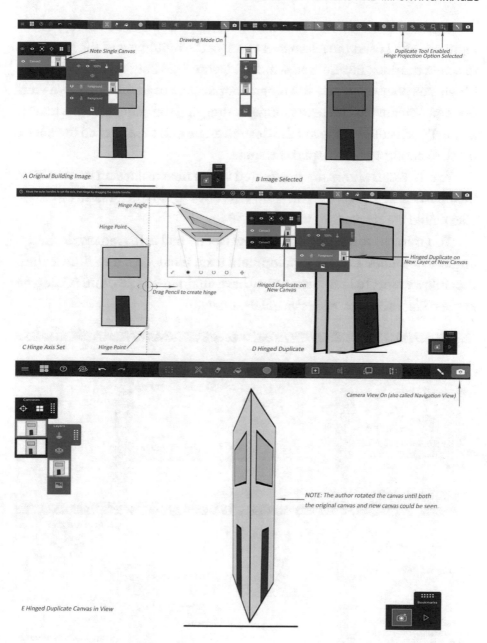

Figure 5-26. *Using the Duplicate tool to create a hinged duplicate*

Figure 5-26A shows we began with a single canvas of a building. In Figure 5-26B, I used the Lasso tool to select the building and the Brush tool to select the door, façade, and window. Figure 5-26C shows where I set my hinge axis points to create the hinged duplicate. I used the Bird's Eye View Preview Window to create the hinge by dragging the center circle with my Apple Pencil until I achieved the desired angle and then clicked the check mark to confirm and accept the change.

Figure 5-26D shows the duplicated image now resides on its own layer on a new canvas. Figure 5-26E shows the effect from the Camera Mode, also called the Navigation View.

You may be wondering how I knew when I had achieved my desired angle. The Mental Canvas development team included a nice little feature that allows users to know when they have attained 30-, 45-, and 90-degree angles. Figure 5-27 provides visual examples.

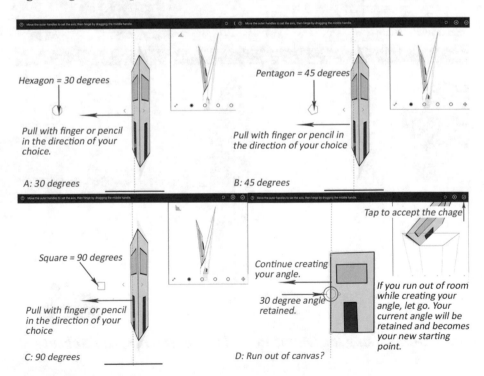

Figure 5-27. *Determining your angle*

As you begin creating your angle by pulling the center circle in your chosen direction, you will notice it changes shape. When it changes to a hexagon, you have achieved a 30-degree angle (Figure 5-27A). When it changes to a pentagon, you have reached 45 degrees (Figure 5-27B), and when it changes to a square, you have attained a 90-degree angle (Figure 5-27C). Nice, right?

And should you run out of canvas as you are creating your desired angle, let go of the center circle. It will pop back to its origin point while retaining whichever angle you have reached. Just continue pulling the circle from that point until you get to your desired angle. Then accept the change and return to *Drawing Mode* by tapping on the check mark (Figure 5-27D).

Importing Layers from External Sources

Besides the ability to import images from sources outside the Mental Canvas application, the Mental Canvas development team gave creatives the ability to create artwork with applications such as Procreate®, Adobe Fresco®, GIMP, and other graphical creation/editing software, and then import all of the layers into Mental Canvas.[6] The benefit of creating artwork outside of Mental Canvas? You have more advanced features and tools available to you than you do inside the Mental Canvas application. However, before you can import, you must first export the layers from your external application.

Figures 5-28 through 5-31 are visual examples of exporting layers from Adobe Photoshop® on a MacBook Pro®.[7]

---

[6] Adobe and Adobe Fresco are registered trademarks of Adobe Inc.; Procreate is a registered trademark of Savage Interactive Pty Ltd. GIMP is open source software and not trademarked.

[7] MacBook Pro is a registered trademark of Apple Inc.

Figures 5-32 and 5-33 are visual examples of exporting layers from Adobe Fresco® on an iPad Pro®.[8]

Figure 5-34 is a visual example of exporting layers from Procreate®.

In actuality, you are not exporting the layers but .png copies of them.

Note: It is beyond the scope of this book to provide instruction on the use of external applications for the production of graphical content. The following figures are used as examples of ways you can export layers from three popular graphics editors.

Exporting Layers from Adobe Photoshop

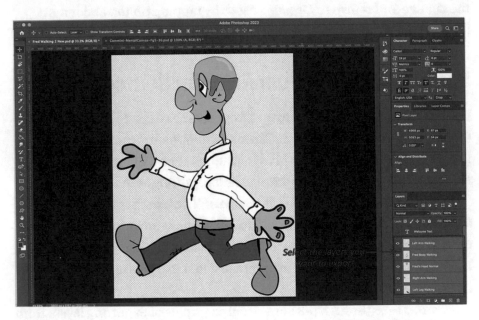

Figure 5-28. *Selecting layers for export from Adobe Photoshop®*

To produce the images for this book, I used Adobe Photoshop® on my MacBook Pro® and Adobe Fresco on my iPad Pro® and dabbled with Procreate®. In Figure 5-28, I selected the layers I wanted to export.

---

[8] iPad Pro is a registered trademark of Apple Inc.

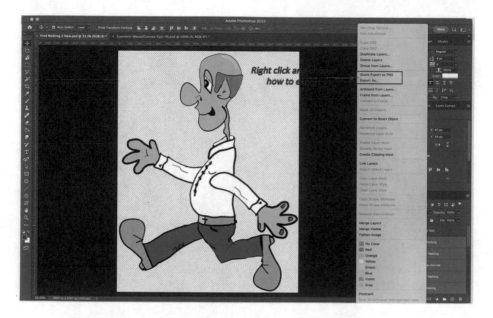

Figure 5-29. *Right-click to choose the export function*

Next, I right-clicked on the highlighted layers and selected the method of export. Figures 5-30 and 5-31 are visual examples of each.

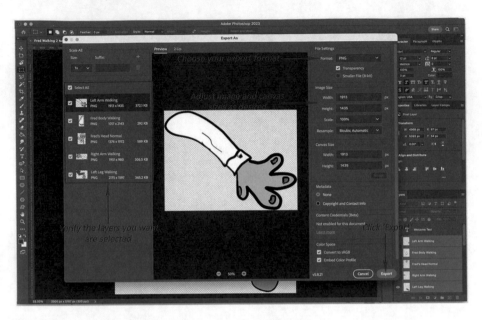

Figure 5-30. *Using the "Export As" method*

Using the *"Export As"* method allows you to choose the export format.
The options are PNG, JPG, and GIF. I recommend exporting in the PNG
format as it saves the images with transparency. *Export As* also gives
creatives the ability to adjust both the image and the canvas sizes in
pixels. You can also add copyright information to the metadata. Once you
have everything adjusted the way you want, click "Export" to move to the
next step.

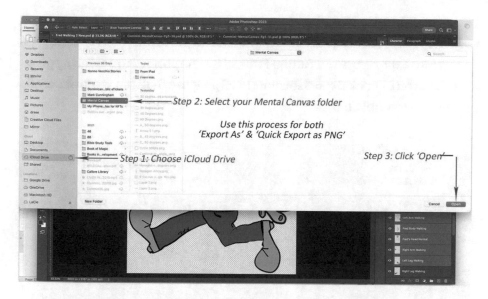

Figure 5-31. *Using the "Quick Export as PNG" method*

Choosing the "Quick Export as PNG" method takes you immediately
to the "Save" window. Here, you choose your export location. In this case,
because the Mental Canvas application only allows importing from the
iPad Pro's photo albums and my MacBook Pro saves my images to iCloud
Photos and not the local Photo app albums, I chose to export to my iCloud
Drive, where I selected the Mental Canvas folder. Clicking "Open" saves
the files to the chosen location and closes the Save window. Note that this
method of saving is used by both the "Export As" and the "Quick Export as
PNG" methods.

Exporting Layers from Adobe Fresco®

Adobe Fresco® is an application available on the iPad Pro. It replaced
the Adobe Photoshop Sketch® and Adobe Illustrator Draw® apps for
mobile devices that allowed raster images (Sketch) and vector images
(Draw). Adobe Fresco allows creatives the ability to select either option.

Figures 5-32 and 5-33 were created using the vector mode. I chose the vector option because the resolution remains the same when resizing.

Before exporting from Adobe Fresco, it is important to set the app up for the correct Quick Export format (PNG). Figure 5-32 is a visual example of how to accomplish this.

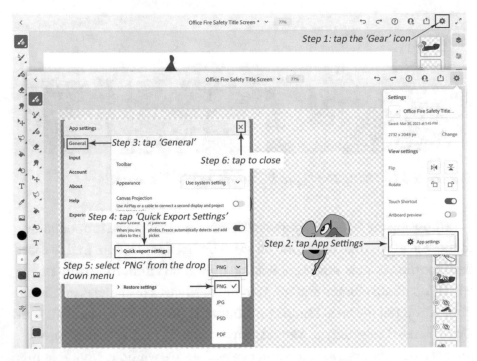

Figure 5-32.   *Setting up Adobe Fresco® for PNG format*

First, from within the Adobe Fresco® workspace, tap the "Gear" icon in the title bar. This will open the "Settings" window. Next, tap the "App Settings" button to open the App Settings pop-up window. Tap "General", then tap the "Quick export settings" arrow to open the format choices. Tap "PNG" to select that file format, and finally, click the "X" in the top right corner of the App Settings window to save the format settings and close the window.

Once you have the Quick Export settings saved, it is time to export your layers.

Figure 5-33. *Selecting layers for export from Adobe Fresco®*

Due to limitations with Adobe Fresco®, you have to export one layer at a time. As you can see from Figure 5-33 "Step 1," to do that, you must choose one layer for export and hide the other layers. Once the layer has been chosen, tap the "Share" icon on the title bar (Figure 5-33 "Step 2").

The steps from there are fairly user intuitive:

1. Tap "Quick Export" (Figure 5-34 "Step 1"). The "Save" window will open.

2. Tap "Save Image" (Figure 5-34 "Step 2").

3. Receive the "Export Complete" confirmation message (Figure 5-34 "Step 3") and repeat the procedure until you have exported all the layers you want to export.

4. Locate your PNG files in the iPad Pro's Photo Album.

5. (Optional) Move the files to a Mental Canvas album.

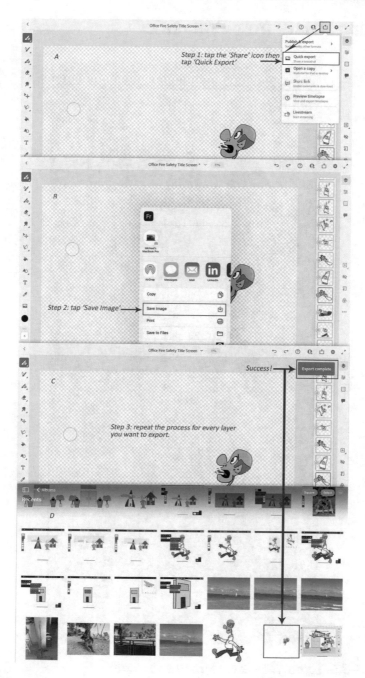

Figure 5-34. *Selecting layers for export from Adobe Fresco®*

Exporting Layers from Procreate®

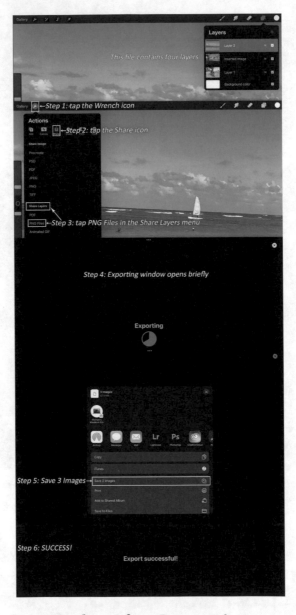

Figure 5-35. *Exporting layers from Procreate*®

Exporting layers from Procreate® is a straightforward process. Please refer to Figure 5-35 for a visual representation:

1. Step 1 – Tap the Wrench icon to open the "*Actions*" panel (Figure 5-35 "Step 1").

2. Step 2 – Tap the "Share" icon.

3. Step 3 – Tap the "*PNG Images*" in the "Share Layers" menu.

4. Step 4 – A window will open with the message, "Exporting".

5. Step 5 – Tap "Save X number of Images". (**Note**: Do not tap "Save to Files" unless you are saving to an external device.)

6. Step 6 – Congratulations! You have successfully exported your PNG files to your iPad Pro's Photo Album.

Moving Files to Your iOS Photo Album

Recall from the cover page to Part 3 that iOS places limitations on how Mental Canvas can import images. Specifically, it can only do so from the iOS Photo Album. As a result, you must move the .png files you exported from your external image editing application from the export location you chose to the Mental Canvas photo album you created in the iOS Photo app. Figures 5-36 and 5-37 are visual examples of how to do that.

The easiest way to transfer the files is to use the *Split View* feature included with every iPad Pro® manufactured in late 2015 onward.[9] I used the most recent version of iPadOS (v. 16.4). If you have an older version,

---

[9] According to the Apple Wiki located at `https://apple.fandom.com/wiki/Split_view`

you can go to the Apple Support page that includes instructions for using split view with your version of iPadOS. At the time of writing, the available choices are iPadOS 13, iPadOS 14, iPadOS 15, and iPadOS 16.[10]

Remember I exported files from two devices: my MacBook Pro® to my iCloud Drive® and my iPad Pro®. As a result, there is an additional step to import the files exported from the MacBook Pro®. Figure 5-36 provides a visual walk-through of the process.

Step 1: Moving Files from iCloud Drive®

Begin by opening the files app on your iPad Pro and navigate to location for your exported images. In this case, because I exported files from my MacBook Pro® to my iCloud Drive®, I opened my files app, tapped on iCloud Drive®, and selected the Mental Canvas folder I created earlier.

Next I selected the .png files I wanted to move to my photo album, created a Mental Canvas album in my iPadOS Photos app, and placed all the image files into this album.

---

[10] https://support.apple.com/guide/ipad/open-two-items-in-split-view-ipad08c9970c/13.0/ipados/13.0

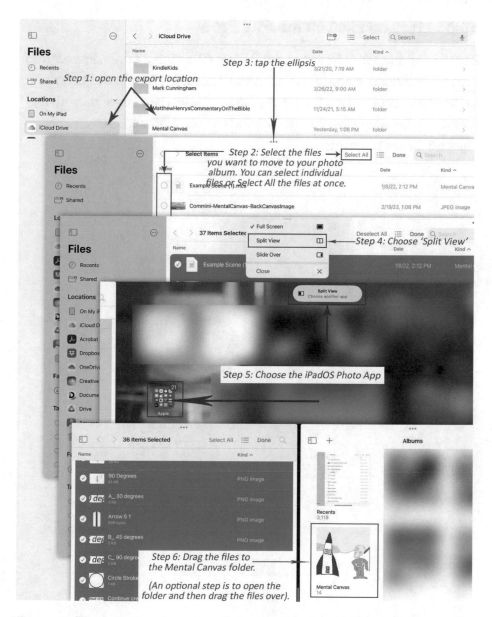

Figure 5-36. *Moving the exported .png files from iCloud Drive to the iOS Photo Album*

Step 2: Moving Files on the iPad Pro®

Recall I exported files from two graphics applications: Adobe Fresco® and Procreate®. Because both applications reside on my iPad Pro®, I exported to the same location: my iPad Pro® photos application. I then moved the files from the main album to the Mental Canvas folder created earlier. Figure 5-37 is a visual guide.

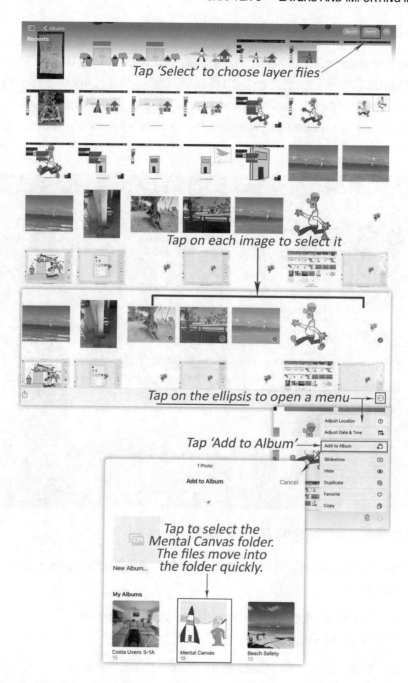

Figure 5-37. *Moving the exported .png files on the iPad Pro®*

Step 3: Importing the Files into Mental Canvas

Finally, we come to the part in the process where we bring the layer images into Mental Canvas. As Figure 5-38 demonstrates, the process is identical to importing single images with the exception that you can choose to import multiple images simultaneously as either a *Layer Stack* or a *Canvas Stack*.

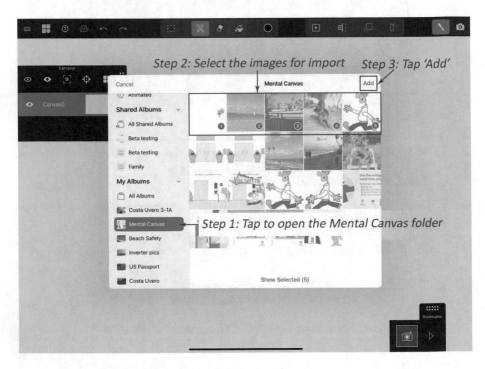

Figure 5-38. *Importing layer images*

Figure 5-39 shows a visual example of bringing the images in as a Layer Stack.

1. Select the images to import into Mental Canvas (refer to Figure 5-38).

2. Choose to bring them in as a Layer Stack (refer to Figure 5-39A).

3. The layer images are imported into Mental Canvas
    on their own layers on the same canvas (refer to
    Figure 5-39B).

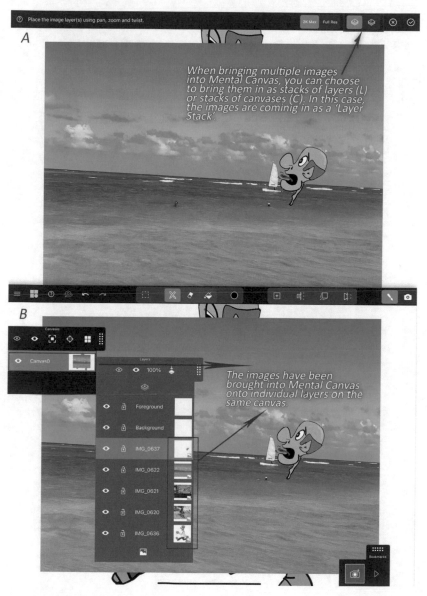

Figure 5-39. *Importing a Layer Stack*

Figure 5-40 shows a visual example of bringing the images in as a Canvas Stack.

1. Select the images to import into Mental Canvas (refer to Figure 5-38).

2. Choose to bring them in as a Canvas Stack (refer to Figure 5-40A).

3. The layer images are imported into Mental Canvas on their own canvases (refer to Figure 5-40B).

Figure 5-40. *Importing a Canvas Stack*

Congratulations, you have completed the layer images importation!

Summary

In this chapter, we learned how to add layers to our Mental Canvas project and how to add and edit images, including canvas placement, explored the use of a Mental Canvas template, and learned the importance of canvas projection to place each image in 3D space to achieve the effect we wanted, and we learned how to add layers from external applications. Additionally, we learned how to import layer images as both Layer Stacks and Canvas Stacks.

In the next chapter, we will explore the use of bookmarks to

- Save specific camera views

- Use those views to return us to proper camera orientation when necessary

- Use bookmark timing to allow us to build fly-through animation effects

Practical Exercises

- Open an existing scene or create a new one.
- Locate the Layers Panel on the left-hand side of your device's screen.
- If it is open, tap it to minimize it. Tap it again to close it. Tap it once more to open it.
- Familiarize yourself with the tools across the top of the layers panel.:
  - Hiding and unhiding layers
  - Layer opacity
  - Creating new layers
  - Image Import
  - Layer Image Import
  - Duplication tools
- Long press one of the thumbnails in the *Layers Panel* to open the sub-menu and select either *Rename* or *Delete* to rename or delete the layer accordingly.

CHAPTER 6

Bookmarks, Timings, and Animation

In the last chapter, we learned how to add, edit, and manipulate new layers, how to import and manipulate images, and also how to import layers into Mental Canvas from external applications such as Adobe Photoshop®, Adobe Fresco®, and Procreate®.[1]

---

[1] Adobe, Adobe Photoshop, and Adobe Fresco are registered trademarks of Adobe Inc. Procreate is a registered trademark of Savage Interactive Pty Ltd.

© Michael Commini 2023
M. Commini, *Mental Canvas for Training and Development*,
https://doi.org/10.1007/978-1-4842-8774-3_6

In this chapter, we will explore the use of bookmarks and timings to create animated effects such as panning and fly-through. We will also examine the video creation and export process used to finalize your Mental Canvas presentation.

Here are this chapter's objectives.

By the end of this chapter readers will know how to:

    a.   Use Bookmarks to:

          i.   Create *Key Views* called *Bookmarks*.

         ii.   Use those *Key Views* to animate their scenes

    b.   Use *Bookmark Timings* to create animation effects.

    c.   Finalize their *Mental Canvas* project and export the video presentation.

    d.   Finalize their *Mental Canvas* project and *Publish to Web*.

A Word About Working in 3D Space

Before we explore the use of bookmarks and timings to animate our *Mental Canvas* presentations, a brief review of working within 3D space is necessary.

Every creative is familiar working within 2D space and the limited depth or perspective with which we can produce our designs. We are limited to *Height*, the *Y-Axis*, or *Up and Down*, and *Width*, the *X-Axis*, or *Left to Right*.[2] Examples of 2D objects include, but are not limited to, paintings, photographs, drawings and sketches, and computer graphics such as icons and logos.

In *Mental Canvas*, a third plane is introduced. Called the *Z-Axis*, this plane represents the *depth* of an environment and is the *front to back* orientation. It intersects with the X and Y axes. If you were to plot the planes on a graph, the point at which all three planes intersect would have the coordinates of 0, 0, 0. Called the *Cartesian Coordinate Method*, the first 0 represents the X-Axis, the second 0 represents the Y-Axis, and the third 0 represents the Z-Axis.

Examples of 3D objects include, but are not limited to, sculptures, architectural models, and the computer graphics used in video games such as World of Warcraft®, Call of Duty®, and The Elder Scrolls® Online.[3] Figure 6-1 shows examples of 2D and 3D objects,[4] and Figure 6-2 shows a visual representation of a Cartesian Coordinate graph.

---

[2] This section is based on Commini (2012), *Rapid Simulation and Game Development for Beginners with Thinking Worlds Version 3.6.0* and modified for the Mental Canvas application.

[3] World of Warcraft is a registered trademark of Blizzard Entertainment, Inc. Call of Duty is a registered trademark of Activision Publishing, Inc. The Elder Scrolls is a registered trademark of ZeniMax Media Inc.

[4] Images retrieved from www.metmuseum.org/art/collection/ and are in the public domain.

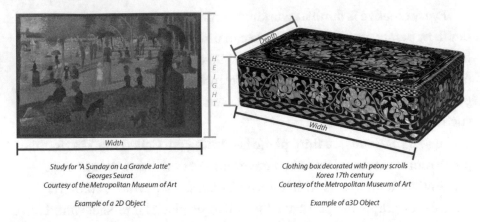

Study for "A Sunday on La Grande Jatte"
Georges Seurat
Courtesy of the Metropolitan Museum of Art

Example of a 2D Object

Clothing box decorated with peony scrolls
Korea 17th century
Courtesy of the Metropolitan Museum of Art

Example of a3D Object

Figure 6-1. *Examples of 2D and 3D objects*

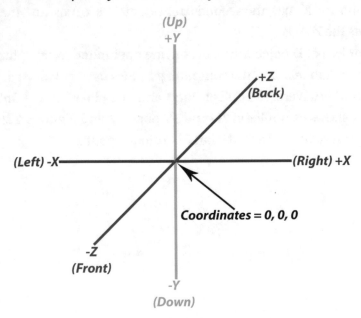

Figure 6-2. *The planes in 3D space[5]*

---

[5] Taken from Commini (2012), *Rapid Simulation and Game Development for Beginners with Thinking Worlds Version 3.6.0.*

In previous chapters, we learned Mental Canvas was made to allow creatives to work with 2D sketches, images, and drawings inside 3D space. As a result, this means we now have the ability to place those sketches, images, and drawings on their own canvases at any point within a 360° radius on each axis. Figure 6-3 provides a visual representation.

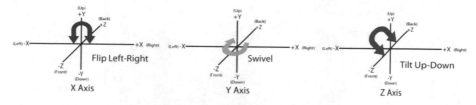

Rotation About the Axes

Figure 6-3. *Working in 3D space on each axis[6]*

On the X-Axis, we can move our canvases within a 360° radius from left to right. On the Y-Axis, we can move our canvases within a 360° radius up and down. And on the Z-Axis, we can rotate our canvases within a 360° radius from front to back. Just think of the possibilities available to us when projecting our canvases within our work products!

Of course, it also means we can get lost when working with multiple canvases. So how do we maintain the proper perspective so our final presentation makes sense?

Bookmarking to the Rescue!

As you can see in Figure 6-4, when in *Drawing Mode* within the *Mental Canvas* environment, the canvas on which you are working is always facing the Camera. As a result, it is easy to become disoriented, losing track

---

[6] Ibid.

of where each canvas is in relation to the other canvases. This is where *bookmarks* become one of the most useful features with the Mental Canvas application.

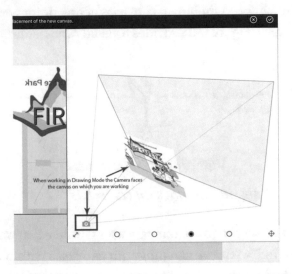

Figure 6-4. *The Camera faces the canvas on which you are working*

Much as your word processing software uses versioning to allow you to return to a previous point, bookmarking at key points provides a point of reference to which you can return. Dr. Dorsey, the creator of *Mental Canvas*, calls these *key views*.[7]

Saving key views at significant points in your project helps you maintain the proper orientation when projecting your canvases, such as when hinging them. When you find yourself becoming disoriented, or discover some other type of error, simply use the bookmarks to return to the key view taken just before you lost your focus and make your corrections. Essentially, each bookmark is a snapshot of your work at specific points in your design (see Figure 6-5).

---

[7] Dorsey, J. 2021. Webinar: Creating Interactive Comics with Mental Canvas

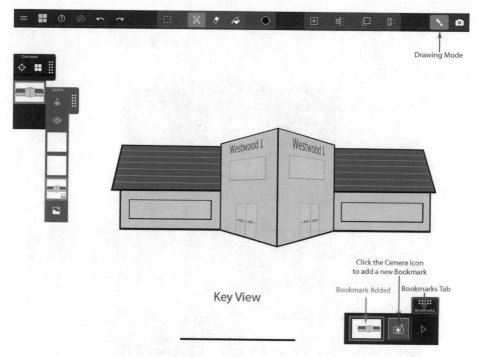

Figure 6-5. *Bookmarking a key view*

For example, when projecting a canvas using the *Hinge* tool, should you find your perspective with the hinged canvas out of alignment with your other canvases, or discover another type of error, simply choose the bookmarked view closest to the point at which you lost your perspective and make your correction (see Figure 6-6).

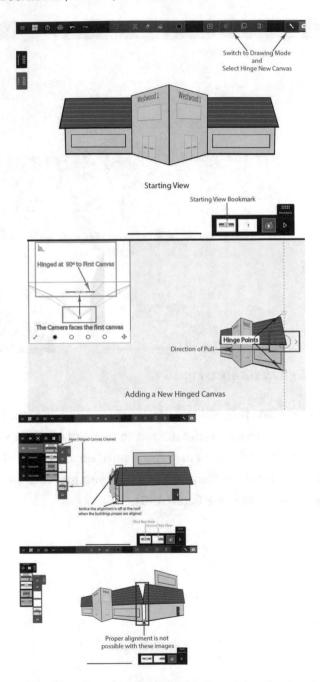

Figure 6-6. *Alignment error identified when hinging a new canvas*

As you can see in the image, when I attempted to hinge a new canvas and align a new image to the original picture, it became apparent that no matter where I moved the new canvas, it was not possible to achieve a perfect alignment as long as the roofs were slanted.

Figure 6-7 shows that changing the roof on the building side (the second canvas) served only to identify that the roofs would not align properly. Using the Canvas Projection tool to push the second canvas back led to the discovery that the roofs in both images would have to be changed altogether.

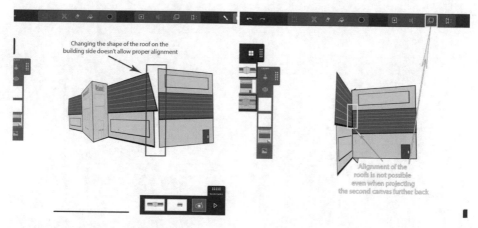

Figure 6-7. *Alignment was not possible with slanted roofs*

In each case of trial and error to get the alignments to work, I used the first bookmark, the first key view, to return to the starting point. This is because Mental Canvas is "view centric rather than object centric."[8] This allowed me to return to the correct viewpoint from which I wanted to work. View centricity allows you to concentrate on "what views of the scene you'll want to use or share and then develop your content accordingly."[9] Figure 6-8 shows the final result.

---

[8] Mental Canvas (2019), *Tour a Tower* Tutorial
[9] Ibid.

Bookmarking at key points also allows you to create animations, which makes your final presentations more engaging and interesting. Using the options available to us on the *Bookmarks Bar*, we can create animated fly-throughs, zooming through our 2D designs in 3D space. We can hide canvases and reveal them at specific points in our presentation – allowing us to provide micro-learning on the go, as it were. And yet the Bookmarks Bar is one of the simplest-to-use tools in *Mental Canvas*. Figure 6-9 provides a visual walk-through of each option.

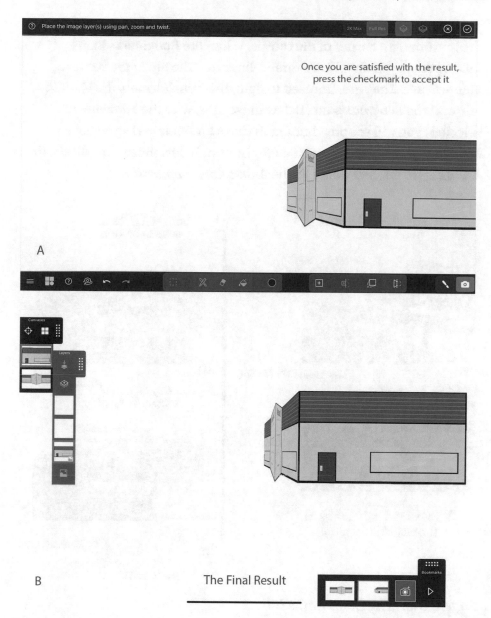

Figure 6-8. *Bookmarking allowed for proper alignment*

To open the *Bookmarks Bar*, tap the *Bookmarks tab* located at the bottom right corner of the canvas. When the Bookmarks Bar is fully opened, you should see three tabs across the top of the bar (see Figure 6-9A). They are, from left to right, the *Timelines* tab, the *Visibility* tab, and the *Bookmarks* tab. Below those tabs, with the *Timelines* tab selected, you will see any thumbnail views for bookmarks you have created, the *Camera* icon, and a *Play* button. Below those you will see the *Animation Timing* sliders and the *Animation Loop* button.

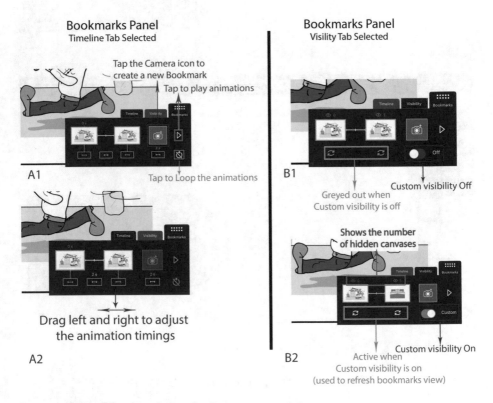

Figure 6-9. *The Bookmarks Bar*

When the *Visibility* tab is selected, you will see, from the top down, the icons showing the number of hidden canvases, any bookmarks you have created, the *Camera* icon, and the *Play* button. Below those you will find the *Bookmark Refresh* buttons and the *Custom Visibility* toggle switch. The default position for the toggle switch is *Off*. Notice with this switch *Off*, the *Refresh* buttons are grayed out and the first bookmark is shown in all bookmark thumbnail views.

When the toggle is activated, it will turn blue and the word *Custom* will appear, indicating you are in the *Custom Visibility* mode, and the *Bookmark Refresh* buttons will become active. You will also notice that each bookmark now appears in the bookmark thumbnail views. In case it is not yet obvious, the *Custom Visibility* mode is how we control which canvases are visible and which are hidden.

Note   If at any time you wish to delete a bookmark, from either the Timelines or Visibility tab, long press on the bookmark and let go. The option to Delete will appear above the bookmark. Tap it and the bookmark will be removed (see Figure 6-10). Should you decide to keep the bookmark after the word Delete appears, simply tap anywhere on the screen to turn that option off.

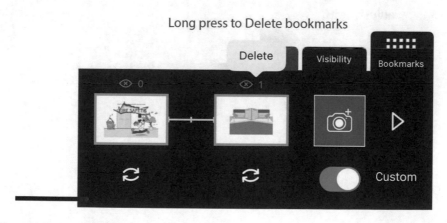

Figure 6-10. Deleting bookmarks

Using Bookmarks to Create Animations

Timeline Tab

Once you have your bookmarks created, you use them to create animations such as zoom-ins, zoom-outs, and fly-throughs. We will cover this more in depth in the project chapters. Here, for your convenience, is a brief explanation for doing this:

- First, navigate through your scene using each key view you have created. If the key view is still relevant to your presentation, keep it. If it's not, delete it and create a new key view representing what you want your audience to see in your final presentation.

- After you have all of the relevant key views, adjust your animation timings. Similar to MS PowerPoint®,[10] Prezi®,[11] and other presentation software, this is more or less trial and error until you have the timings you want for each key view. Press the *Playback* button to test your timings. Figure 6-11 is a visual example of timing adjustment.

---

[10] PowerPoint® is a registered trademark of Microsoft Corporation.

[11] Prezi is a trademark of Prezi, Inc. All rights reserved.

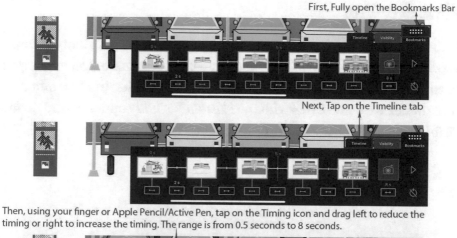

First, Fully open the Bookmarks Bar

Next, Tap on the Timeline tab

Then, using your finger or Apple Pencil/Active Pen, tap on the Timing icon and drag left to reduce the timing or right to increase the timing. The range is from 0.5 seconds to 8 seconds.

Use the Playback button to run your animation and check your timings.

Figure 6-11. *Adjusting animation timing*

Use the *Loop* icon to enable or disable animation looping (see Figure 6-12).

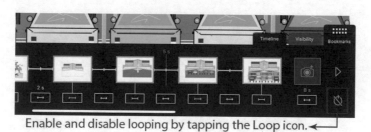

Enable and disable looping by tapping the Loop icon.

Figure 6-12. *Enabling/disabling animation looping*

Visibility Tab

While creating our animations, *Mental Canvas* gives us the ability to turn the visibility of each canvas on and off at will. For example, you might want all canvases visible (on) for some bookmarks but hidden (off) for other bookmarks. We control this with the *Custom Visibility* option found on the *Visibility* tab of the *Bookmarks Bar*,[12] as seen in Figure 6-13.

---

[12] Mental Canvas (2022), Using Visibility Tools to Animate the Flythrough. Retrieved from `https://youtu.be/XdRieVMp-z4`

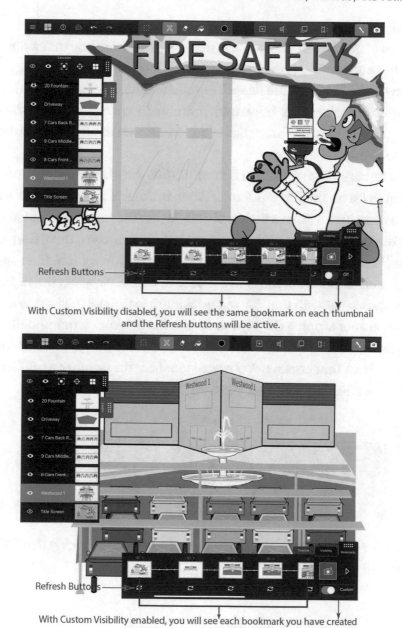

Refresh Buttons

With Custom Visibility disabled, you will see the same bookmark on each thumbnail and the Refresh buttons will be active.

Refresh Buttons

With Custom Visibility enabled, you will see each bookmark you have created and the Refresh buttons will be active.

Figure 6-13. *Enabling/disabling Custom Visibility*

The *Custom Visibility toggle* is found on the *Visibility* tab of the *Bookmarks Bar*. When the option is disabled, the same bookmark appears in all the thumbnails for the bookmarks you have created, reflecting that all canvases are *On* and the *Refresh buttons* are inactive (grayed out). When the option is enabled, the bookmark thumbnails change to reflect the key views you have created throughout your scene, and the *Refresh buttons* become active.

It is important to note that *Custom Visibility* works in conjunction with the canvas list on the *Canvas Panel*. When the toggle is disabled (off), all the canvases in the canvas list are visible. When the toggle is enabled (on), select the bookmark for which you want to hide canvases; then, from the canvas list on the *Canvas Panel*, select the canvas you want hidden and tap the *Eye icon* to the left of the canvas name to hide it. Last, tap the *Refresh button* associated with the affected bookmark to update the key view.[13], [14]

Notice after tapping the *Refresh button* the bookmark thumbnail changes to reflect only those canvases in view for that bookmark and the number above that bookmark changes to reflect the number of hidden canvases for that key view (see Figure 6-14).

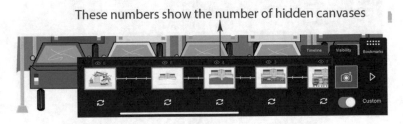

Figure 6-14. *The number above the affected bookmark reflects the number of hidden canvases*

---

[13] Make sure you tap the *Refresh button* and not the bookmark itself so you do not return to the bookmark view.

[14] Mental Canvas (2022), Using Visibility Tools to Animate the Flythrough. Retrieved from https://youtu.be/XdRieVMp-z4

Once you have completed your changes, tap the *Playback button* to verify everything is as you want it. You are now ready to share your presentation.

Sharing Your Scene

Two Options

The *Mental Canvas* team has given us two ways to share our presentations: (1) *Exporting* and (2) *Publish to Web*, which allows us to take advantage of the *Mental Canvas* web player. In this section, we will explore both options.

Export

As seen in Figure 6-15, to export your presentation, you tap the *hamburger menu*. I suggest that you first tap *Save* to save your work and then tap the *Export* submenu to open the *Export Settings* window (see Figure 6-16). Here, you will notice that there are two export options: we can export as *video* for use on YouTube™, Vimeo®, Vevo®, your organization's LMS, or some other form of video delivery,[15] or we can export as a series of *screenshots* for use in a *PowerPoint®* presentation, an *Adobe® PDF* training manual, or some other media format.[16]

---

[15] YouTube is a trademark of Google LLC. Vimeo is a registered trademark of Vimeo.com Inc. Vevo is a registered trademark of Vevo LLC.

[16] PowerPoint is a registered trademark of Microsoft Corporation. Adobe is a registered trademark of Adobe Inc.

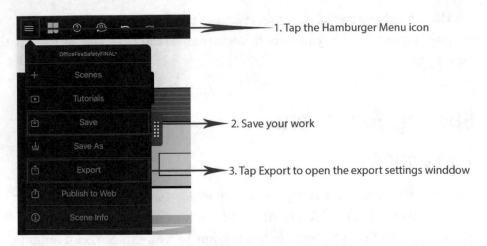

Figure 6-15. *Exporting your presentation*

The settings you select in the *Export Settings* window determine how your presentation appears in whichever export method you choose, video or screenshot, and include the ability to export in *landscape* or *portrait* orientation. As seen in Table 6-1, video *resolution* choices are dependent on the chosen *aspect ratio*.

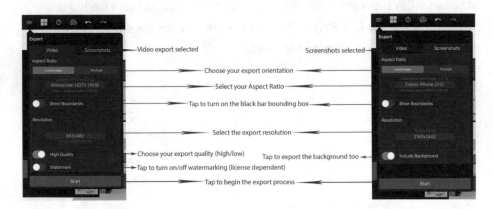

Figure 6-16. *Exporting as video and screenshots comparison*

Table 6-1. *Available video resolutions based on the chosen aspect ratio*

Video Export Resolution Settings per Aspect Ratio			
Landscape		Portrait	
Aspect Ratio	*Resolution*	*Aspect Ratio*	*Resolution*
Square (1:1)	480×480 720×720 1080×1080	Square (1:1)	480×480 720×720 1080×1080
Standard TV (4:3)	640×480 960×720 1440×1080	Portrait TV (3:4)	480×640 720×960 1080×1440
Classic iPhone (3:2)	720×480 1080×720 1620×1080	Classic iPhone (2:3)	480×720 720×1080 1080×1620
Widescreen HDTV (16:9)	853×480 1280×720 1920×1080	Portrait HDTV (9:16)	480×853 720×1280 1080×1920
Ultra-widescreen (21:9)	1120×480 1680×720 2520×1080		

Table 6-2 shows the *resolution* choices available when you export *screenshots*.

Note   When saving screenshots, you lose the ability to choose export quality or to watermark but you gain the ability to include or exclude the *Background*.

Table 6-2. *Screenshot resolution settings based on the chosen aspect ratio*

Screenshot Export Resolution Settings per Aspect Ratio			
Landscape		Portrait	
Aspect Ratio	Resolution	Aspect Ratio	Resolution
Square (1:1)	480×480 720×720 1080×1080 1440×1440	Square (1:1)	480×480 720×720 1080×1080 1440×1440
Standard TV (4:3)	640×480 960×720 1440×1080 1920×1440	Portrait TV (3:4)	480×640 720×960 1080×1440 1440×1920
Classic iPhone (3:2)	720×480 1080×720 1620×1080 2160×1440	Classic iPhone (2:3)	480×720 720×1080 1080×1620 1440×2160
Widescreen HDTV (16:9)	853×480 1280×720 1920×1080 2560×1440	Portrait HDTV (9:16)	480×853 720×1280 1080×1920 1440×2560
Ultra-widescreen (21:9)	1120×480 1680×720 2520×1080 3360×1440		

Showing Aspect Ratio Boundaries

You may have noticed the toggle for *Show Boundaries* in the middle of the *Export Settings* window. *Aspect Ratio* dependent, when enabled, the software places a black bounding box around your video/screenshots similar to what you would see on your Smart TV[17] (see Figure 6-17).

---

[17] Smart TV is a registered trademark owned by LG Electronics Inc.

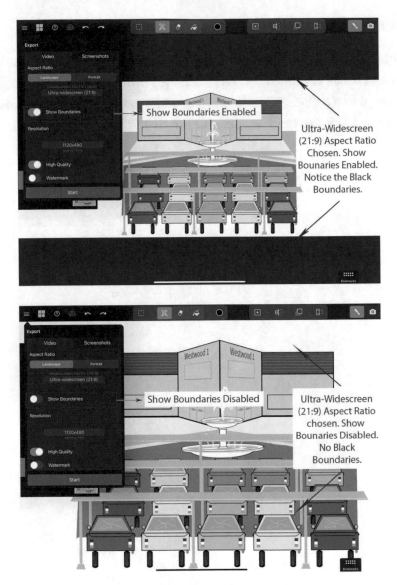

Figure 6-17. *Comparison: Show Boundaries Enabled vs. Disabled*

Publish to Web

The second method for sharing your finished presentation is *Publish to Web*. Depending on the license you chose when you downloaded *Mental Canvas*, you can publish one or more scenes to the *Mental Canvas* website.[18] This allows you to take advantage of the *Mental Canvas* web player, which in turn allows viewers to interact with the scene as an immersive experience: to enter, travel through, and view the scene in countless different ways. The player can be viewed on any web-enabled device, including phones, tablets, and computers.[19]

Figure 6-18 shows the licensing options available at the time of writing and the associated number of public and private scenes that can be published to the Web.

Figure 6-18. *Licensing options and the number of scenes that can be published to the Web*

---

[18] Mental Canvas (2022), *How to Publish to Web*. Retrieved from `https://youtu.be/BuOZKXQvxZ4`

[19] Mental Canvas (2016-2022). Retrieved from `www.mentalcanvas.com/products/web-player`

As you can see, the *Promo* license only allows watermarked video export. The *Creator* license allows you to publish one *Public* web scene. When you publish your scene under this license, it goes into a publically accessible gallery. This means that anyone can see it.[20]

The *Education* and *Professional* licenses allow you to publish "up to 5 public or private interactive web scenes."[21] Scenes published under these licenses remain private by default. To make them publically available, contact the *Mental Canvas* team. The private links can be shared with anyone you wish. This means you can create your scenes, publish to your private gallery on the *Mental Canvas* site, and share them with your organization who can then experience your presentations as engaging, interactive training interventions!

The *Enterprise* license is a multi-seat plan. Contact *Mental Canvas* for more details and to purchase this license.[22]

Figure 6-19 presents a set of visual instructions for publishing scenes to the Web.

---

[20] Ibid.

[21] Retrieved from www.mentalcanvas.com/purchase

[22] Ibid.

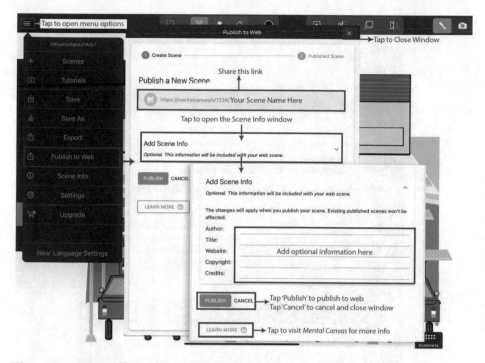

Figure 6-19. *Follow these instructions to Publish to Web*

1. Tap the *hamburger menu* icon to open the menu options.

2. Tap Publish to Web to open the *Publish a New Scene* window.

3. Give your scene a name. Copy the link and share it once the scene has been published.

4. (Optional) Add Scene Info to include author's name, title, website (if applicable), copyright information, and applicable credits.

5. Tap *Cancel* to cancel and close the window.

6. Or tap *Publish* to publish to the link created in step 3. Figure 6-20 contains screen grabs of publishing a scene in progress.

Figure 6-20. *Publishing to Web in progress – success!*

Figure 6-21 shows that once the scene has been published, it will appear in the *Publish a New Scene* window with the options to

- Replace or rename one of the previously published scenes

- Copy to clipboard

- Open the scene in the *Mental Canvas* web player

- Delete the scene from your device and the Mental Canvas gallery

Figure 6-21. *Modifying or deleting scenes*

Finally, Figure 6-22 shows the test scene in the Mental Canvas web player. (The test link was deleted after taking the screenshot.)

Figure 6-22. *The published test scene in the Mental Canvas web player*

Summary

In this chapter, we reviewed what it means to work in *3D space* and learned about a feature provided by the *Mental Canvas* team called *key views*, or *bookmarks*. We explored using bookmarks as anchor points, allowing us to return to a specific key view in cases of making errors, wanting to add canvases to that view, or otherwise editing canvases and layers in that view.

We also explored using bookmarks to create animations such as fly-throughs by adjusting the animation timings on the *Bookmarks Bar Timeline* tab and using the options on the *Bookmarks Bar Visibility* tab in conjunction with the *Canvas Panel* to affect canvas visibility during scene playback.

Finally, we examined the two methods of sharing our finalized scenes: Exporting videos and screenshots and Publish to Web.

This concludes the informational section of the book. Chapters 1 through 6 were written to provide readers with the knowledge necessary to begin developing their skills using the *Mental Canvas* application. The next section provides projects by which readers can further develop their skills and build experience designing and constructing scenes for use in an organization's training and development program.

Practical Exercises

If you have not yet done so, use all of the knowledge gained from chapters one to six to:

- Create a scene for use in your organization's training & development program. Be sure to use Key Views
  - o Use at least one Key View to add a Parallel Projected Canvas
  - o Use at least one Key View to add a Hinged Canvas
- Experiment with the options on the Bookmarks Bar Timeline and Visibility tabs to
  - o Create animated flythroughs
  - o Hide/unhide canvases during animation playback
- Save your scene
- Export your scene as either
  - o A video
  - o A series of screenshots
- Publish your scene to the web and share it with others in your organization

In Her Own Words – Snow Wi

My name's Snow. I'm used to be called like this abroad for all my life since this is how my name sounds like and what it means in Russia where I'm originally from, so I took this direct translation of my name as an artist's name.

I work as a freelance artist for 3 years for now, creating magic by my hands and selling it as canvases and NFTs, creating different kinds of visual assets for writers, musicians, bloggers, actors, businessmen and other people all around the world.

This love for art have been with me since I remember myself, I have been passionate about it since early age. All the kinds of creativity were my loyal companions at all the stages of life, but drawing remained a special place among them.

Trying new ways of expressing myself, my thoughts, feelings and experiences, broadening the creative horizons always excited me, therefore I never limited myself in materials, styles, tools and other things that could help me to bring the world in my mind to reality. So I always find the ways to improve my skills, to learn something new and to move further.

This is how I've found Mental Canvas.

In the first place it looked like a nice toy to play with my digital paintings and bring some fresh vision into them. But the more I discovered the software the more opportunities of using it I started to see, and they inspired me for absolutely new things.

By that time I worked on developing my TikTok character Jenny that I used for frame based animations. And one day the craziest idea hit me - I decided to create a house for her. Mental Canvas seemed to be an ideal and easy instrument for implementing this idea.

I planned it to be a great digital asset that I could use as a decoration for my animations. I got that inspired that I literally sat for days and nights in front of my iPad and laptop being obsessed with the process.

I studied the plans of the houses and modified them in a easier way for me to use, studied interior design so I could create something really nice and cozy. Many materials, references and sources were worked out before the actual work on the house started.

It took me over 1,5 months of actual hard work to finish the project. For drawing the assets and details I used Procreate app where I was used to work already, then I imported them to mental canvas.

I've faced many technical struggles that really stressed me out and even made me frustrated sometimes such as the lack of the memory of my old iPad, huge weight of the project in general that caused lots of lags. My poor laptop was almost dying praying for mercy. But I got really lucky to have such a great team of mental canvas being always nearby ready to help me with all the kinds of problems I had. They kindly solved all the technical issues and were just really supportive in general. I'm still truly thankful to them and I hope we'll continue cooperating in future!

So Jenny's house that seemed to be just an insane idea in the beginning was done! There are 2 floors and 6 complete rooms there including the kitchen, living room, little art studio, secret Winchester's room, game room, bedroom and bathroom.

It turned to be not just a digital decoration but a true manifestation of my own dream house and a whole digital place for so many needs and events!

For the last year I've already used the house as a digital gallery for my fancy NFT collection, as a background for the animation as I planned in the beginning, and even for a huge online new year party with my artist friends that I'm going to repeat this year!

One of the greatest things I like about it is that I can always change and edit everything I need - there can be any season of the year "set", any object added or removed. And the whole project can be even turned into an interactive web3 space that is so important to me as an NFT artist!

So, thanks to this incredible program I got just a fantastic digital platform of mine!

Besides the Jenny's house I've used Mental Canvas for other professional needs too. I've created custom presentations, greeting videos and ads, promo cartoons and animations.

Mental Canvas is one of my obligatory working tools now and I absolutely love it!

...

Best regards,

S.W.

SECTION IV

Projects

CHAPTER 7

Project 1: Office Fire Safety Part 1

In the previous chapters, we explored and learned how to use the tools provided by the *Mental Canvas* application that enable creatives to take 2D sketches, drawings, and images and place them into 3D space, thus allowing us to create engaging, interactive presentations.[1]

Through a series of lessons in this chapter and the next, we will apply what we have learned and build an *Office Fire Safety* presentation for use in an office safety training environment. We will walk step-by-step through the design process using the image files I have created specifically for this project.

Here are this chapter's objectives.

---

[1] Using the Mental Canvas web player.

M. Commini, *Mental Canvas for Training and Development*,
https://doi.org/10.1007/978-1-4842-8774-3_7

Objectives

In this chapter readers will:

a. Follow step-by-step to begin creating a training intervention using the Mental Canvas application.

b. Develop their skills adding canvases, layers and images.

c. Develop their skills merging layers and projecting merged layers onto new canvases.

d. Develop their skills duplicating layers.

Note   Except for those images provided by the *Federal Emergency Management Agency* (FEMA), all images in this project were created by me and are copyrighted. You may use them with limited permissions. Proper crediting of the author is required.[2] FEMA is a US government agency. The images provided by FEMA are in the public domain.

---

[2] If you use the supplied author-created images, please reference the author as Commini, M.F. (2023), *Mental Canvas for Training and Development: Creating Engaging, Interactive Presentations* (1st ed). Apress.

Accessing the Files

If you have not yet done so, please download and install the image files and place them into an iOS/iPadOS[3] Photo Album titled *Project 1 – Fire Safety*. Refer to Cover Page 3 if you need help. Figures 7-1 through 7-4 show a list of the files you should have.[4]

---

[3] iOS is a registered trademark of Cisco Systems Inc. and is used under license. iPadOS is a registered trademark of Apple Inc.

[4] **Note**: Due to a quirk with the iOS/iPadOS file naming system, your file names may change when you import the images. Figures 7-1 through 7-4 are provided for your reference.

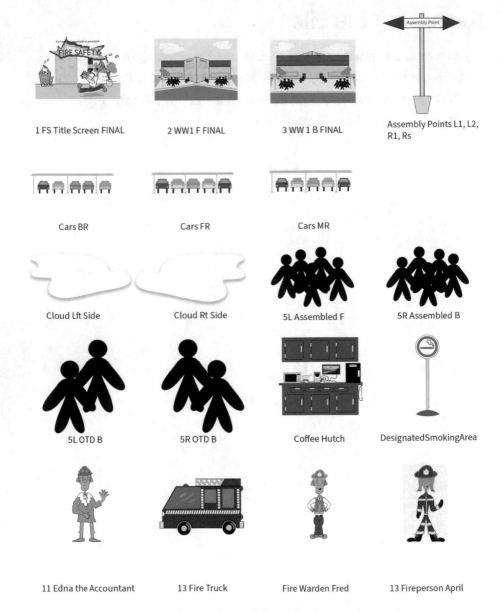

1 FS Title Screen FINAL

2 WW1 F FINAL

3 WW 1 B FINAL

Assembly Points L1, L2, R1, Rs

Cars BR

Cars FR

Cars MR

Cloud Lft Side

Cloud Rt Side

5L Assembled F

5R Assembled B

5L OTD B

5R OTD B

Coffee Hutch

DesignatedSmokingArea

11 Edna the Accountant

13 Fire Truck

Fire Warden Fred

13 Fireperson April

Figure 7-1. *The list of images used in this chapter, part 1*

Figure 7-2. *The list of images used in this chapter, part 2*

Figure 7-3. *The list of images used in this chapter, part 3*

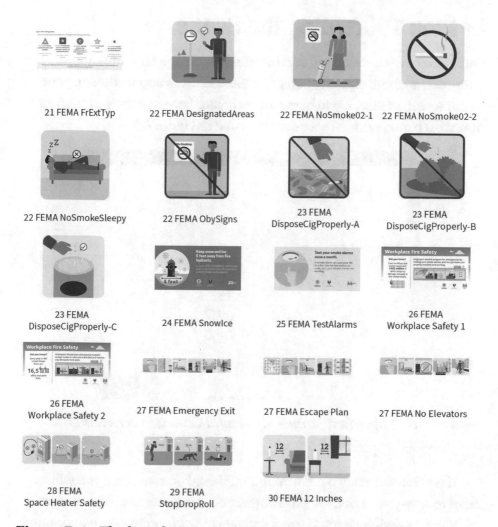

21 FEMA FrExtTyp

22 FEMA DesignatedAreas

22 FEMA NoSmoke02-1

22 FEMA NoSmoke02-2

22 FEMA NoSmokeSleepy

22 FEMA ObySigns

23 FEMA
DisposeCigProperly-A

23 FEMA
DisposeCigProperly-B

23 FEMA
DisposeCigProperly-C

24 FEMA SnowIce

25 FEMA TestAlarms

26 FEMA
Workplace Safety 1

26 FEMA
Workplace Safety 2

27 FEMA Emergency Exit

27 FEMA Escape Plan

27 FEMA No Elevators

28 FEMA
Space Heater Safety

29 FEMA
StopDropRoll

30 FEMA 12 Inches

Figure 7-4. *The list of FEMA images used in this chapter*

Disclaimer: The projects developed in this chapter are abridged versions of possible training interventions. They are not intended to be full training sessions. Rather, they are designed to allow you to begin building your skills in *Mental Canvas* and provide an idea of training interventions you can use with your own peers.

Lesson 1: Creating the Scene

Once you have downloaded and installed the image files into the appropriate photo album, open the *Mental Canvas* application on your touch screen device. If you have not yet created any scenes, your app will open to a blank, untitled scene such as that in Figure 7-5

Figure 7-5. *When first launched, Mental Canvas opens with a blank scene*

If you have already been working in *Mental Canvas*, then you will need to save your work. We have already covered how to do that in earlier chapters. I provide Figure 7-6 as a convenience to you in case you skipped those chapters or would like a reminder.

Refer to Figure 7-6A: Tap the *hamburger menu* and choose either *Save As* (if you have not yet saved your work) or *Save* (if you have already named your scene).

If you have not yet saved your work, choose *Save As*. Give your scene a name and place it in whichever location you prefer (Figure 7-6B).

If you have already named your scene, choose *Save* and then decide whether to *Discard* or *Save* your changes (Figure 7-6C).

Once your changes have been saved or discarded, tap the hamburger menu again and select *Scenes* (Figure 7-6D).

The File Manager window will open, allowing you to tap the + sign. Doing so will open the *Templates* window. Choose a template, give your new scene a name, and tap *Done* (Figure 7-6E).

Your new scene will open (Figure 7-6F).

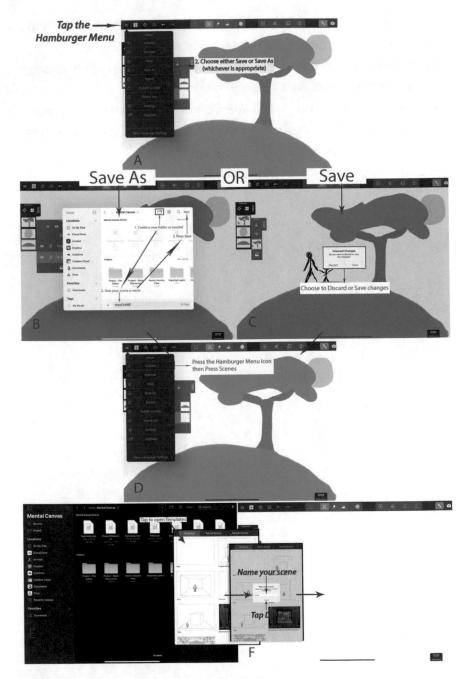

Figure 7-6. *First, save your work and then create your scene*

Once your new scene is open, double-check to be sure you are in *Drawing Mode* and begin drawing or adding images, canvases, and layers.

As previously mentioned, *Mental Canvas* creates the scene with one canvas and two layers. You can choose to work only on this canvas, or you can choose to take advantage of working in 3D space and add more canvases and layers.

Lesson 2: Adding the Files

Earlier in this book, we learned that *Mental Canvas*, while powerful in its own right, provides a limited graphics editor. For more exacting work, you might wish to take advantage of other drawing applications such as Adobe Photoshop®, Adobe Fresco®, GIMP, or Procreate®.[5] For this project, I chose to create the artwork in Adobe Photoshop® and Adobe Fresco®.

This chapter will assist you in developing and practicing your skills adding canvases, layers, and images to build a presentation on *Office Fire Safety*. You will also practice exporting that presentation as a stand-alone video for use in your organization's Learning Management System (hereafter, LMS) or as an interactive presentation for use with the *Mental Canvas* player via the *Publish to Web* feature.

Adding Your First Canvas

We will begin by adding the title screen to the canvas. Figure 7-7 provides visual step-by-step instructions.[6]

---

[5] Adobe, Adobe Photoshop, and Adobe Fresco are registered trademarks of Adobe Inc. Procreate is a registered trademark of Savage Interactive Pty Ltd. GIMP is open source and not trademarked.

[6] **Note**: I updated the image file names after the figures for this chapter were created. The file names in the figures may not match the new file names.

1. We begin with a blank canvas and verify we are in *Drawing Mode.*

2. Next we open our Canvas and Layers Panels.

3. Notice the image icon under the background layer? Tap it to open your iPad's photo albums and select the *Project 1 – Fire Safety* album you created in a previous chapter.

4. Locate the *Fire Safety Title Screen FINAL* image and tap it to select it.

5. Now tap *Add* to import the image to your *Mental Canvas* application.

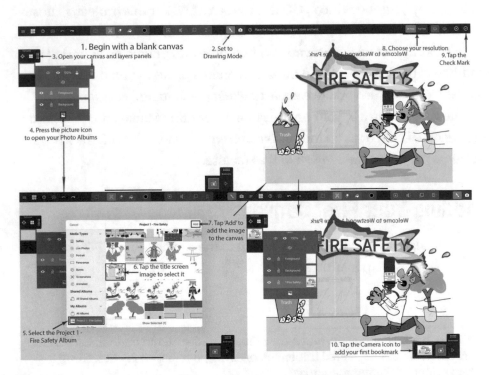

Figure 7-7. *Adding the first project image to the canvas*

6. Once the image is imported, choose the resolution you wish to use. Recall from a previous chapter that bringing in full resolution images can have negative effects on the performance of your device and/or the application.

7. Finally, tap the *Camera* icon to add your first bookmark.

Next, we are going to add a *New Canvas* parallel to and behind the title scene canvas. Figure 7-8A through D provides a visual walk-through of the steps required.

1. Begin with the first canvas in view. Make sure you are in *Drawing Mode* (Figure 7-8A).

2. Tap the *New Canvas Tool* icon and use the *Preview Window* to assist in placement of the new canvas *behind* the first canvas. As previously discussed, you can move and resize the *Preview Window* as needed. You can also use the viewing buttons at the bottom of the *Preview Window* to find the best angle from which to observe your positioning efforts (Figure 7-8B).

Figure 7-8. *Adding a new projected canvas*

3. With your finger or your Apple Pencil (or active pen for Windows users), push up on the canvas in the main window to move it behind the first canvas. Once you have it positioned where you want it, tap the *check mark* to accept it (Figure 7-8B).

4. You will be returned to the main canvas where you will open the Layers Panel for the new canvas and tap the *Image icon* (Figure 7-8C).

5. Locate the *4FAA Westwood 1* image in the *Project 1 – Fire Safety* photo album and select it. Then press *Add* to add the image to the new canvas (Figure 7-8D).

6. If given a choice, choose your desired resolution and tap the *check mark* to accept it (Figure 7-8D).

7. Hide the Title Screen canvas to check the placement of the new canvas (Figure 7-8D).

Figure 7-9 is a screenshot of the Main Canvas with both canvases unhidden and *Custom Visibility **Off***. Notice that you only see a thumbnail of the first canvas in the *Bookmarks* thumbnail windows.

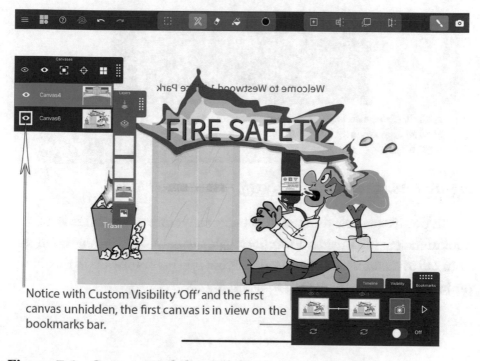

Notice with Custom Visibility 'Off' and the first canvas unhidden, the first canvas is in view on the bookmarks bar.

Figure 7-9. *Custom Visibility Off, first canvas unhidden*

Figure 7-10 is a screenshot of the same window. This time, however, the first canvas is hidden. Again, *Custom Visibility* is ***Off***. Notice the title scene canvas is now in every thumbnail.

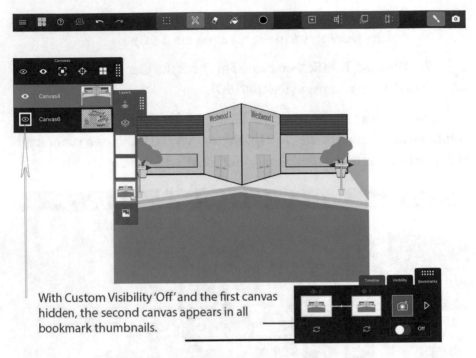

With Custom Visibility 'Off' and the first canvas hidden, the second canvas appears in all bookmark thumbnails.

Figure 7-10. *Custom Visibility Off, first canvas hidden*

To be able to see a thumbnail of every canvas for which there is a bookmark, tap the *Custom Visibility* toggle to enable it. The label changes from *Off* to *Custom* (see Figure 7-11). From this point forward in this project, please work with *Custom Visibility **On***.

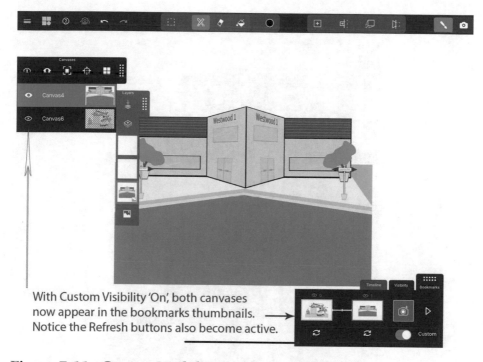

With Custom Visibility 'On', both canvases now appear in the bookmarks thumbnails. Notice the Refresh buttons also become active.

Figure 7-11. *Custom Visibility On, first canvas hidden*

Lesson 3: Repositioning Canvases (1st Rabbit Trail)

What if the position of the new canvas is not quite where you want it? What can you do to correct it? Figure 7-12 shows you step-by-step how to resolve the issue.

1. First, make sure you are in *Drawing Mode* (Figure 7-12A).

2. Select the canvas on which you wish to work from the Canvas Panel (Figure 7-12A).

3. Tap the *Selection* icon to enter *Editing* mode (Figure 7-12A).

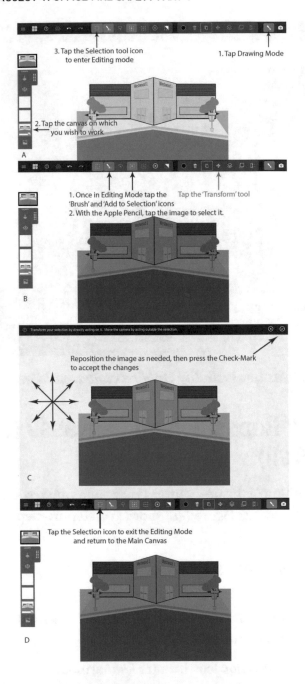

Figure 7-12. *Repositioning a canvas*

4. Tap the *Brush* and *Add to Selection* icons
   (Figure 7-12B).

5. Tap the image you want to reposition with your
   Apple Pencil (your active pen for Windows users)
   (Figure 7-12B).

6. Tap the *Move* tool (Figure 7-12B).

7. Reposition your image as needed and then tap the
   check mark icon (Figure 7-12C).

8. Finally, tap the *Selection tool* icon to exit
   Editing mode.

Lesson 4: Keeping Your Canvases and Layers Organized (2nd Rabbit Trail)

As you add layers and canvases, it will become very easy to get lost during
the design process. This is especially true if you rely on the names the
Mental Canvas app automatically assigns when you add them. For this
reason, you should consider renaming your layers and canvases and
saving your work periodically. Thankfully, the Mental Canvas development
team gave us an easy way to change layer and canvas names.

Renaming Layers

To rename your layers you (refer to Figure 7-13):

1. Long press on the layer name and release to open
   the submenu.

2. Tap *Rename* to open the *Rename Layer* text box.

3. Give the layer a new, meaningful name. A meaningful name will help you quickly locate the layers should you wish to make any changes or use the *Opacity* tool to duplicate characters for animations.

4. Tap *Done* to close the text box and complete the renaming process.

5. The new name appears on the layer.

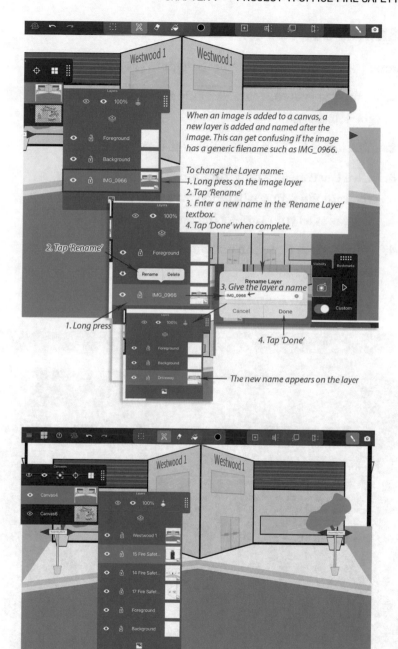

Figure 7-13. *Renaming a layer*

Renaming Canvases

To rename your canvases you (refer to Figure 7-14):

1. Long press on the canvas name and release to open the submenu.

2. Tap *Rename* to open the *Rename Canvas* text box.

3. Give the canvas a new, meaningful name. A meaningful name will help you quickly locate the canvases as your project becomes large and bulky.

4. Tap *Done* to close the text box and complete the renaming process.

5. The new name appears on the canvas.

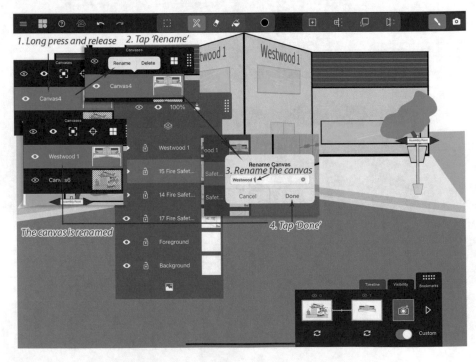

Figure 7-14. *Renaming a canvas*

Reorganizing Layers and Canvases

Another way we can organize our layers and canvases is by moving the layers and canvases up and down within their respective panels. Where layers are concerned, this has an effect similar to what you are familiar with in applications such as Adobe Photoshop®, Adobe Fresco®, Procreate®, and GIMP.

Layers

Using layers, we can place one image atop another. Depending on the position of the content you place on the layers, the layer on top can either let you see the layer below or hide it. Figure 7-15 is a visual example of layers stacked one atop the other.

Notice on the Mental Canvas screenshot I have one canvas with two layers. The layer with the house is above the layer with the hill. From this example, it is easy to see that the house obscures part of the hill. This is because of its layer positioning.

To further explain the effect of layer positioning, I took a screenshot of the *Mental Canvas* screenshot from within Adobe Photoshop®. Notice the text that begins "With the house layer..." sits above both the house and the hill. Again, this is because of its position within the Adobe Photoshop® layer list. By moving layers around, we can achieve some interesting effects for our projects. For example, we can use the *Opacity* tool to onion-skin the layer below, thus enabling ourselves to create duplicates of its content. This is useful when animating characters.

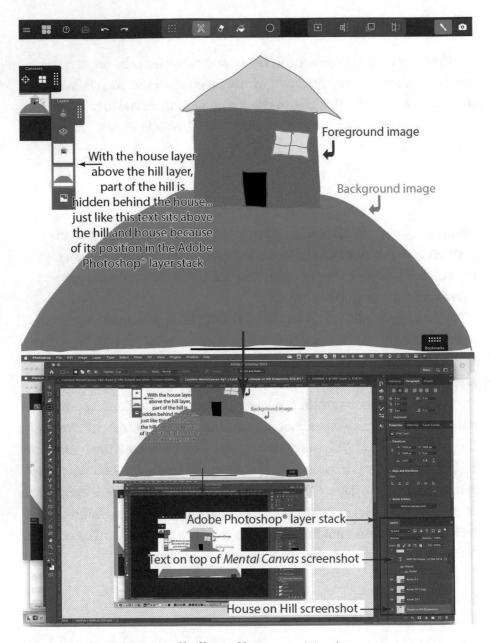

Figure 7-15. *The overall effect of layer positioning*

By now, you are familiar with the long press and release feature the *Mental Canvas* developers provided for renaming and deleting. A similar feature is used for repositioning layers and canvases. As Figure 7-16 demonstrates, locate the layer or canvas you wish to move, long press and drag it up or down in the list. When you have reached your desired new location, let go.

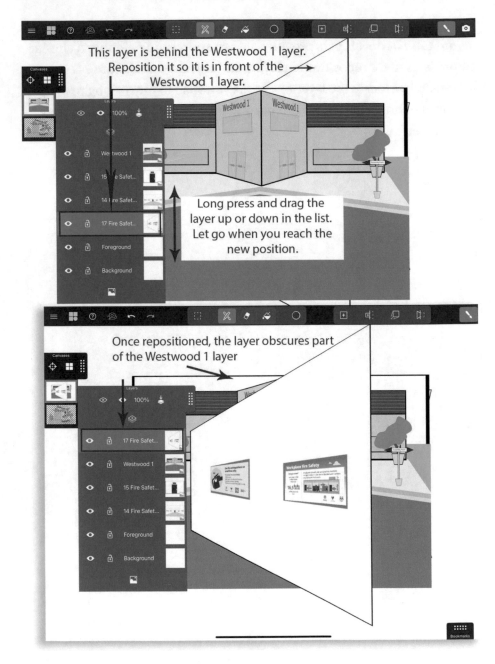

Figure 7-16. *Repositioning layers*

Canvases

Unlike working with layers, it does not matter where in the list we place our canvases. "This is because the visibility of a canvas is based on where it is in our scene."[7] Moving a canvas up or down in the list will not make a difference for what you see because the canvases themselves have not been moved[8] (see Figure 7-17).

---

[7] Mental Canvas (2022), *Working with Layers*, retrieved from https://youtu.be/knV-2buHy_k

[8] Ibid.

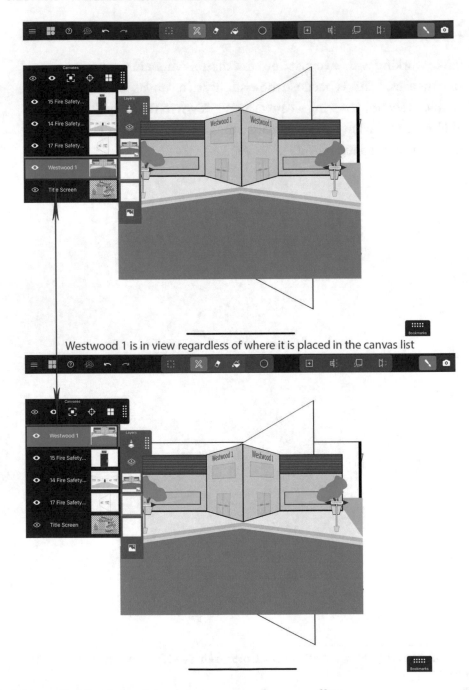

Westwood 1 is in view regardless of where it is placed in the canvas list

Figure 7-17. *Repositioning canvases has no effect*

In fact, the only reason for repositioning canvases in your list is to organize them in an order meaningful to you and your workflow.[9] Reorganizing the canvases in your list follows the same process as reorganizing your layers. Long press on the canvas you want to move and drag it to your desired position in the list. Figure 7-18 provides a visual example.

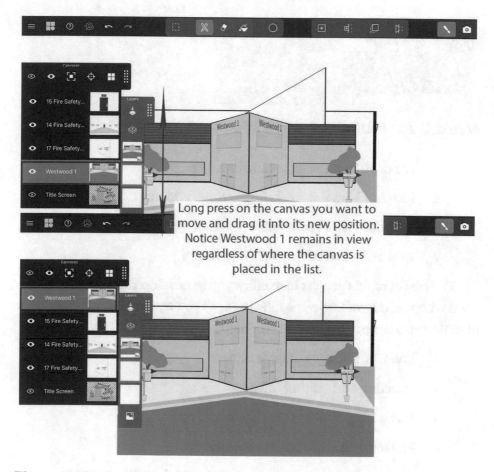

Long press on the canvas you want to move and drag it into its new position. Notice Westwood 1 remains in view regardless of where the canvas is placed in the list.

Figure 7-18. *Long press the canvas and drag it up or down*

---

[9] Ibid.

Lesson 5: Adding More Canvases

As discussed in an earlier chapter, there are multiple ways to add canvases to your scene (see Figure 7-19).

Figure 7-19. *Multiple ways to add canvases*

1. You could tap the *New Canvas* icon.

2. You could tap the *New Hinged Canvas* icon.

3. You could tap the *Canvas Projection tool* icon.

4. You could tap the *Hinged Canvas* icon.

The object of this project is to allow you to develop the various skills used with the *Mental Canvas* application. As you can imagine, there is a lot of material to cover. This project will help you develop skills in

- Importing images onto canvases

- Selecting and editing images

- Manipulating images on layers and canvases

- Projecting images onto new canvases

- Creating hinges to allow your users to take advantage of viewing your final presentation in 3D space

- Bookmarking key views

  - Using those views to create an animated final presentation

  - Adjusting the visibility of those views

  - Adjusting the animation timings

- Exporting your final presentation

Importing Images to Layers

Picking up where we left off before taking the rabbit trails, begin by making sure you are in *Drawing Mode*, the *Title Screen* canvas is hidden, and the *Westwood 1* canvas is selected in your canvas list and is in view. You should have three layers and two bookmarks, and *Custom Visibility* should be enabled. Refer back to Figure 7-11 for a visual reference. If your scene does not match what you see in Figure 7-11, please correct it now. Refer back to Figure 7-8 for guided visual instructions as needed.

Tap the *Image* icon to open the *Photo Album* and choose the *Project 1 – Fire Safety* album. Select the following 14 images:

- 4FAA Westwood 1 (our working file for now)

- 4FA Westwood 1(hide this for now)

- 4FB Westwood 1 (hide this for now)

- 5L Assembled F (hide this for now)

- 5L OTD F (hide this for now)

- 5R Assembled F (hide this for now)

- 5R OTD F (hide this for now)

- 6 Assembly Point (hide this for now)

- 6L Tree (hide this for now)

213

- 6R Tree (hide this for now)

- 7 BR Cars (hide this for now)

- 7 FR Cars (hide this for now)

- 7 MR Cars (hide this for now)

- 20 Fountain

Note   I encountered a five-image limit when importing the images into the *Mental Canvas* scene. If you encounter the same issue, you will need to import multiple times.

Figure 7-20 is a visual review of the image importation process covered in an earlier chapter. It is provided here for your convenience. Recall that when importing images, you have the option of bringing them into the *Mental Canvas* application at either 2K or Full Resolution. Recall also that you can import them simultaneously onto layers of the same canvas or onto multiple canvases.

In this case, you should import them onto multiple layers of the *4FAA Westwood 1* canvas. This will be our base canvas from which we will work. Hide the images as noted in the preceding list. To see all the images you imported onto the canvas, scroll up or down through the *Layers Panel* list.

And now the fun begins! Now we turn our 2D static scene into a 3D journey that will engage our learners! Begin by locking all the layers except for the *20 Fountain* layer. This is so we do not inadvertently change anything on the other layers (see Figure 7-21).

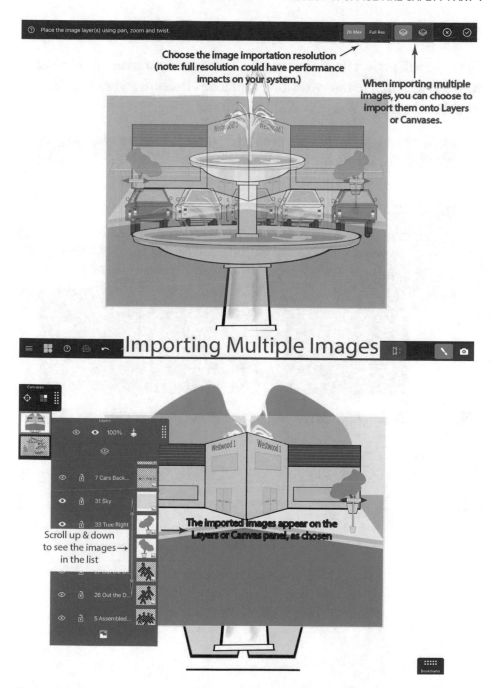

Figure 7-20. *Importing multiple images at the same time*

Projecting Layer Images onto New Canvases

Next, we will project the fountain onto a new canvas, resize it, and position it so it sits in front of the Westwood 1 building. Refer to Figure 7-22 for visual instructions. Figure 7-23 shows the end result.

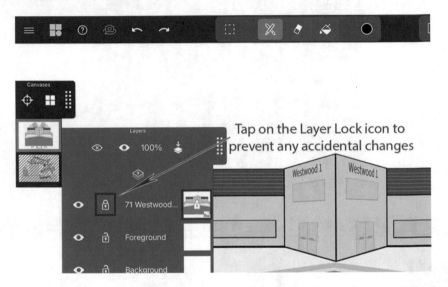

Figure 7-21. *Locking layers to protect them from accidental changes*

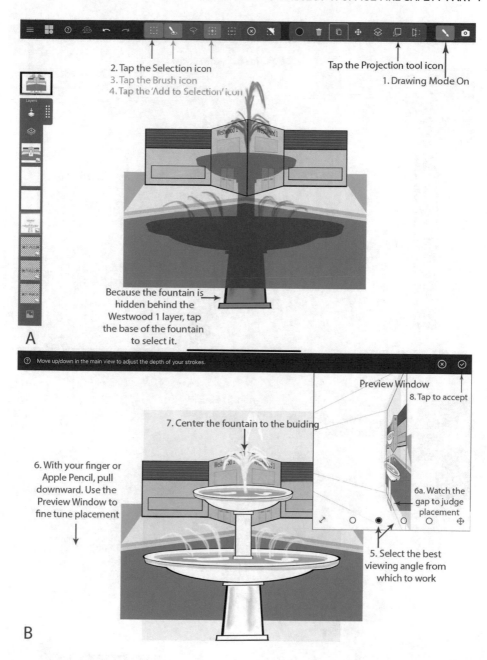

Figure 7-22. *Projecting the fountain onto a new canvas*

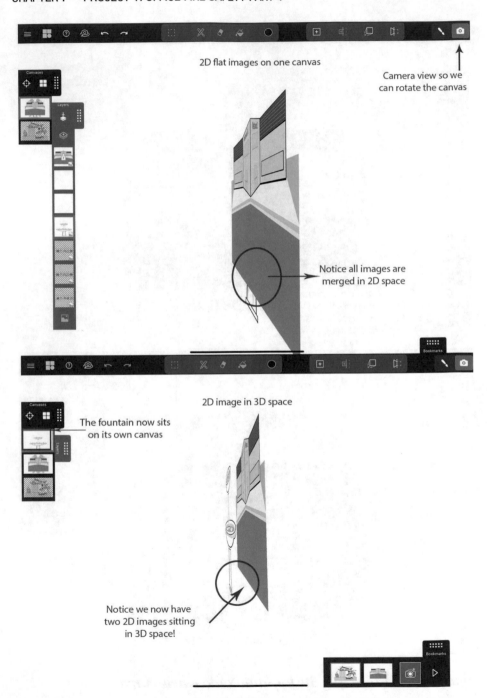

2D flat images on one canvas

Camera view so we can rotate the canvas

Notice all images are merged in 2D space

2D image in 3D space

The fountain now sits on its own canvas

Notice we now have two 2D images sitting in 3D space!

Figure 7-23. *Moving a 2D image into 3D space*

Now we need to resize the fountain so it fits the scale with which we are working. First, create a bookmark to save this view in case you have to return to it (see Figure 7-24). Make sure the *20 Fountain* canvas is selected in the Canvas Panel.

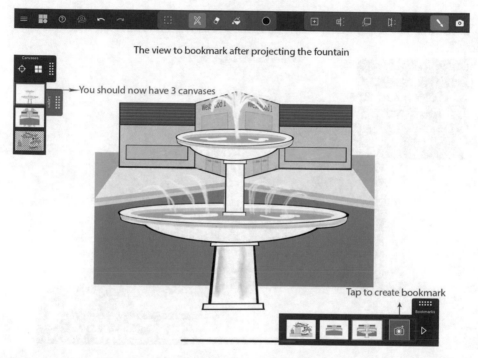

Figure 7-24. *Create a bookmark from this view*

Enter *Drawing Mode* if you are not already there. Then tap the *Selection* icon to open the *Editing* window and tap the *Brush* and *Add to Selection* icons. With your Apple Pencil or active pen/pencil, tap the fountain to select it. Now tap the *Transform* icon.

With the image of the fountain selected, two-finger pinch anywhere on the canvas to resize the image smaller. Be sure to keep it centered with the corner created by the joining of the two front door sections of the building. Finally, move the fountain into the center of the drive and tap the *check mark* to accept the change.

Tap the *Selection* icon to exit *Editing* mode and return to the main canvas. Your canvas should look similar to Figure 7-25. Delete the bookmark you created at the beginning of this process and create a new one from this view.

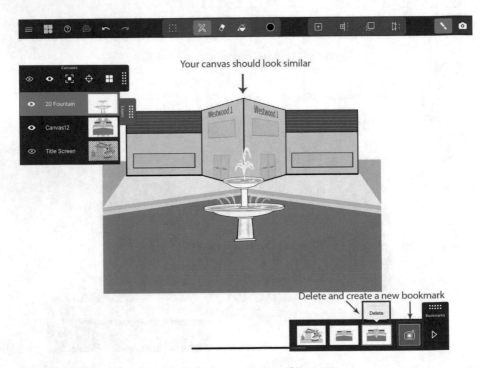

Figure 7-25. *The fountain's new size and position*

You might be wondering why I had you create the bookmark and then delete it, only to create a new one. If for any reason you had to step away from your device or made a mistake, you would have been able to immediately return to this point in your project. The new bookmark saved the new view with the resized and repositioned fountain.

Projecting a Hinged Canvas

By now, you have noticed that the *4FAA Westwood 1* image contains a dark gray area at the bottom of the image. This represents the roadway leading up to the building – in other words, the ground. Because *Mental Canvas* allows us to place our 2D images into 3D space, the development team provided us with an editing tool that allows us to affect changes to our ground plane. Briefly covered in an earlier chapter, that tool is the *Hinge* tool. We will use it here to rotate our ground plane.

1.   First, hide the Fountain and Title Screen canvases, then make sure to select the Westwood 1 canvas (or whatever you named it) in the Canvas Panel list. Open the Layers Panel and select the *4FAA Westwood 1* layer. Lock the other layers and then tap the *Selection* tool to enter *Editing* mode and select the *Lasso* tool. One nice feature provided by the *Mental Canvas* developers is the ability to select straight edges. We do that by drawing semi-circles with the Lasso tool (Figure 7-26A).

2.   Begin by placing the *Lasso* tool at the point where the two yellow lines join, then draw out and around to the edges of the image. Do this for both the left and right sides of the image (Figure 7-26A).

3.   Next use the *Lasso* tool to draw around the remaining exposed section to close the selection (Figure 7-26B).[10]

---

[10] If you have trouble making the selection, make sure you have not locked the Westwood 1 layer.

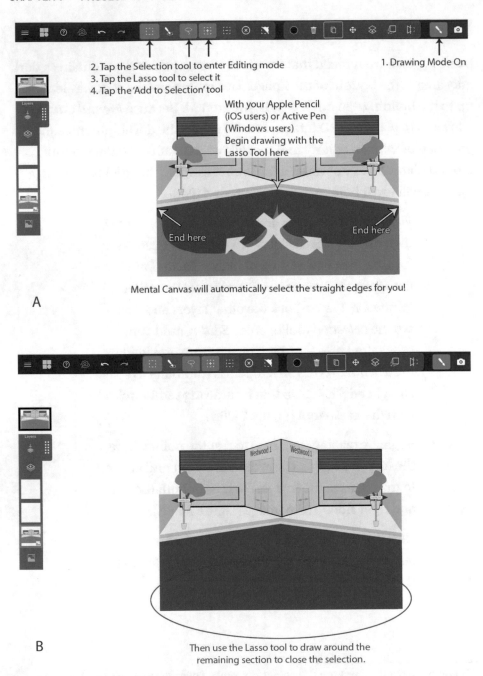

Figure 7-26. *Using the Lasso tool to select straight lines*

222

Once your selection is complete, indicated by the selected area turning red, tap the *Hinge tool* icon (Figure 7-27A). A new window will open showing the canvas with its selection visible in the center of the screen from a top-down viewpoint. Use the *Preview Window* to select different viewpoints until you find the one that is most useful. Figure 7-27B shows a step-by-step example for hinging the selected area onto a new canvas. Those steps are as follows:

1. Place the first *Hinge Axis Point* at the far left side of the image where the dark gray "roadway" meets the yellow curb line.

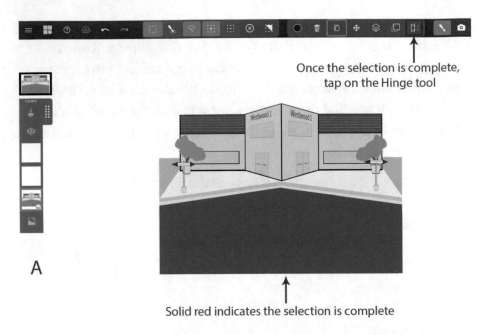

Once the selection is complete,
tap on the Hinge tool

A

Solid red indicates the selection is complete

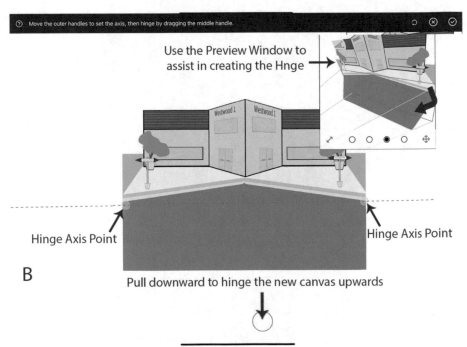

Use the Preview Window to
assist in creating the Hnge

Hinge Axis Point

Hinge Axis Point

B

Pull downward to hinge the new canvas upwards

Figure 7-27. *Creating the hinge*

2. Place the next *Hinge Axis Point* on the other side of
    the image parallel to the first axis point.

3. With your finger or Apple Pencil/active pen, pull
    the circle downward. Watch the canvas rotate in the
    Preview Window until it achieves your desired angle.

4. Finally, tap the *check mark* to accept the changes
    and return to the main canvas.

Once back at the main canvas, unhide the *4FAA Westwood 1* canvas
and tap the *Camera* icon to place a new bookmark. You should now see the
new canvas on the *Canvas Panel* and the new bookmark on the *Bookmarks
Bar*. Rename the new canvas *Driveway* (see Figure 7-28).

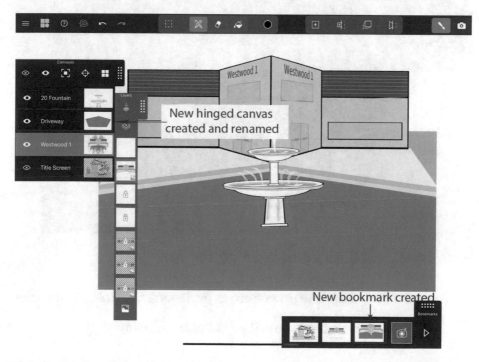

Figure 7-28. *The new hinged canvas: renamed and bookmarked*

Projecting More Layer Images onto New Canvases

Next, we need to project the *7 BR Cars*, *7 FR Cars*, and *7 MR Cars* layers onto new canvases. First, lock and hide the *Westwood 1* layer, then *Unlock* and *Unhide* and select the *7 BR Cars* layer. Remember, it is in the layer list for the *Westwood 1* canvas (see Figure 7-29).

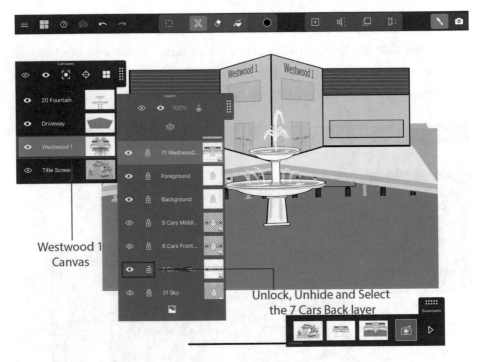

Figure 7-29. *Unlocking and unhiding the layer*

You will follow the same procedure as projecting the *20 Fountain* layer:

1. *Turn Drawing Mode* on, if you have not already done so.

2. Tap the *Selection* icon to enter *Editing mode.*

3. Tap the *Brush* icon.

4. Tap the *Add to Selection* icon.

5. Tap the *Projection* tool icon.

6. In the *Preview Window*, select the best angle from which to view the changes you make. Use the *Preview Window's Move* icon to move the *Preview Window* as needed.

7. With your finger or your Apple Pencil/active pen, push anywhere on the screen to move the *7 BR Cars* layer up or down in relation to the Driveway and Fountain. ***Note:*** You can move the layer 360° in any direction, as desired.

8. Tap the *check mark* to accept the changes once you have the preferred placement (see Figure 7-30 for the placement used by me).

9. Create a new bookmark.

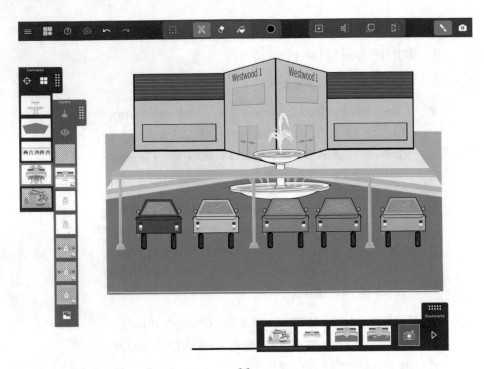

Figure 7-30. *The placement used by me*

Use the skills you developed in the section on *Repositioning Canvases (1st Rabbit Trail)* to move the canvas as necessary, should you need to make any adjustments. Delete and re-create the bookmark if you make any changes. Then, once you are satisfied with the new canvas' placement, follow the same procedure to project *7 MR Cars* and *7 FR Cars* onto new canvases. You *will* need to reposition the canvases to achieve similar placements to mine. Remember to use the *Projection tool,* not the *New Canvas Projection tool,* to move the canvases closer or further away from the canvas before it.

Note   If the layer on which you wish to work is hidden by another layer, hide that other layer as needed (see Figure 7-31).

Once all three layers have been projected onto new canvases, your scene should look similar to Figure 7-32A unless you chose a different placement.

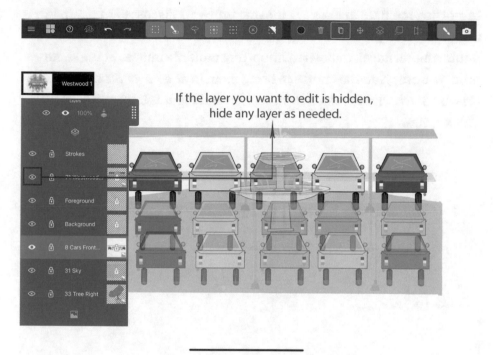

Figure 7-31. *Hide any layers blocking your view*

To see what you have created so far, turn on *Camera View* and use your finger or *Apple Pencil/active pen* to rotate around your scene. Figure 7-32B is a visual example of what you might see. Examine your scene carefully and note any canvas that needs fine-tune adjustments and make them accordingly. Tap your last bookmark to return to the last view and continue building your scene. Remember to go back into Drawing Mode.

You can also tap the *Playback* button to view your work using the default timings.

Importing Multiple Images Simultaneously As Layer Stacks

Importing multiple images at the same time was discussed in depth in Chapter 5 in step 3 of the section on moving files to your iOS/iPadOS[11] photo album. Recall that when importing multiple images at the same time, you are given the choice to bring them in as a *Layer Stack* or a *Canvas Stack*. Please refer to that section and Figures 5-39 and 5-40 for a quick review.

---

[11] I include iOS in the text because users can store and access their photo albums from the desktop, laptop, notebook, and mobile devices. iPhones use iOS as their operating system, and iPad Pros use iPadOS. Both iPhone® and iPad Pro® are registered trademarks of Apple Inc.

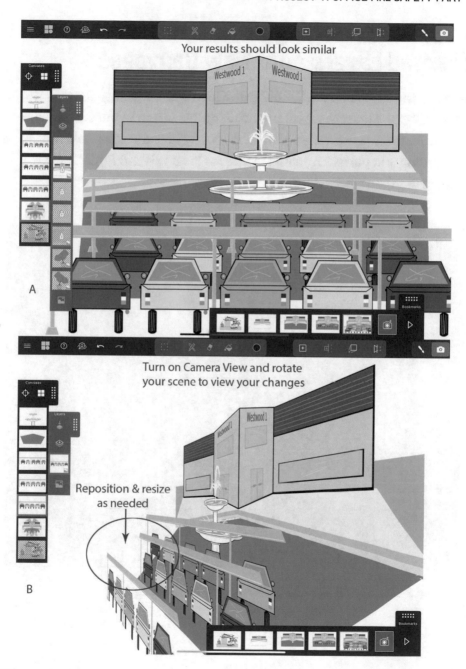

Figure 7-32. *Turn on Camera View and compare your scene to mine*

Lesson 6: Merging Layers and Projecting Merged Layers onto New Canvases

Refer to the 2 *WW1 F FINAL* image provided with the image files (Figure 7-33). Though we will not be using this image in our scenes, you may refer to it to get an idea of my concept for how the scene will look once everything is in place. The same is true for the 3 *WW 1 B FINAL* image (Figure 7-34).

Figure 7-33. *The 2 WW1 F FINAL reference image*

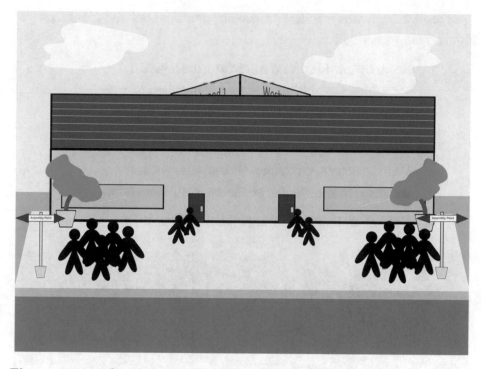

Figure 7-34. *The 3 WW 1 B FINAL reference image*

My concept is for each layer to provide a 3D effect when the scene has been completely built out. To achieve the effects, we will need to merge several layers. Once they have been successfully merged, we will then project them onto their own canvases.

The layers to be merged are as follows:

- 5L Assembled F merged with 5R Assembled F

- 5L OTD F merged with 5R OTD F

- 6L Tree Left merged with 6R Tree Right

Duplicating layers is a straightforward process. Feel free to refer to Figure 7-35, as needed.

1. Begin by unhiding and unlocking the layers. I recommend unhiding and unlocking one layer pair at a time to avoid accidental changes.

2. Tap the *Merge Layers* icon.

3. Verify a successful merge. Hide any layers and canvases to see the merged images, as necessary.

4. Unhide, unlock, and merge the next layer pair.

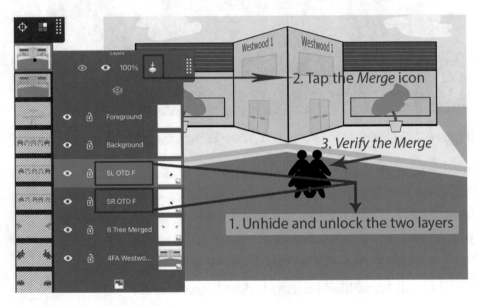

Figure 7-35. *Merging layers*

As you can see, the trees merged one on top of the other. You can use the skills learned in *Lesson 6* to select and resize each image before projecting the layer onto a new canvas or you can project the layer to a new canvas, then select it, resize, and reposition the images.

My Recommendation

With the exception of the merged tree layer, I suggest you project your merged layers onto a new canvas first and then make your changes. Remember to use the *Add to Selection* and *Subtract from Selection* tools when selecting the images. See Figures 7-36 and 7-37 for visual instructions. Remember to unhide the *Westwood 1* canvas before you begin making changes. It really helps being able to see how the overall image is affected.

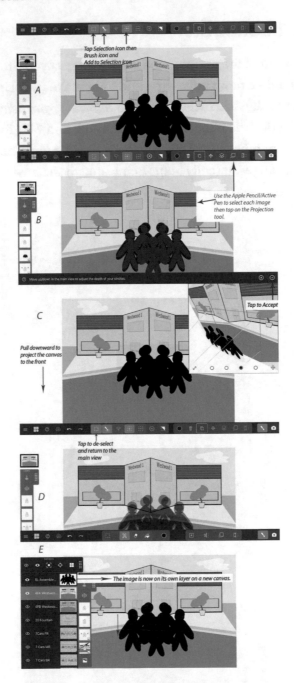

Figure 7-36. *Projecting the merged layer onto a new canvas*

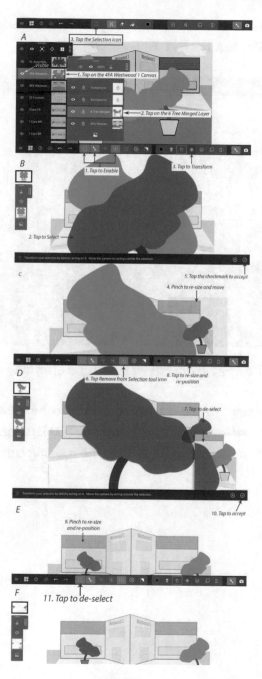

Figure 7-37. *Resizing and moving the images on the canvas*

Use the same process to fine-tune the positions of the images until you have a result similar to mine (see Figure 7-38).

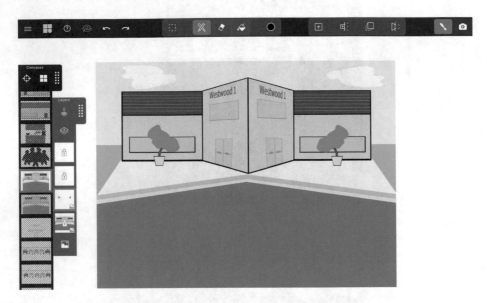

Figure 7-38. *The tree layer resized and repositioned*

Use the same steps to project, resize, and reposition the 5L and 5R Assembled F merged layer and the 5L and 5R OTD F merged layer (see Figure 7-39). Hide those canvases. Repeat the resizing and repositioning steps as needed.

Figure 7-39. *The end result*

Once your scene looks similar, unhide all canvases except the Title Screen canvas and create a bookmark (see Figure 7-40).

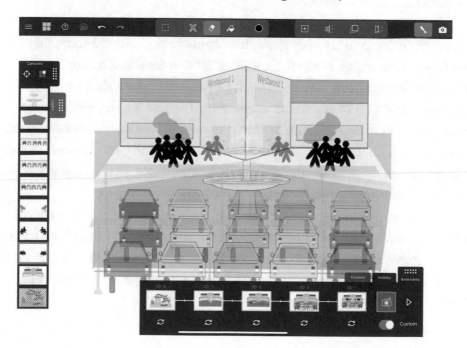

Figure 7-40. *Bookmark created of all canvases in view*

Onion Skinning for Image Placement

During the design of this project, it became apparent that the merged tree layers did not fit the composition I envisioned. Specifically, when the trees were on their own canvas, they stood out too far from the building canvas when rotating around the axis. Therefore, I decided to place the merged trees onto another layer on the *4FA Westwood 1* canvas.

What this means is every instance of the *Westwood 1* canvases needs their own tree layers. This works out well for us because it allows another skill to be developed and practiced, namely, *Onion Skinning*.

For those not familiar with the term, think back to your use of tracing paper in your primary school art classes. When you wanted to create a duplicate of something you had drawn, you would place a translucent piece of paper, called tracing paper, on top of the original image and trace around it, creating a near-perfect duplicate. *Onion Skinning*, as used in *Mental Canvas*, is similar.

As you have discovered by now, *Mental Canvas* is limited in several ways when compared to other graphics applications. For example, there is no *Copy & Paste* tool, nor is there a *Drag & Drop* function, so duplicating the layer and dragging it to a different canvas is not possible. Our only available option is to create instances of the merged tree layers on every canvas and then using Onion Skinning to place those images in exactly the same spot as on the *4FA Westwood 1* canvas. Hopefully, the *Mental Canvas* development team will address this lack in an update. In the meantime, we will use the feature available to us.

To begin, unhide and select the *4FB Westwood 1* canvas. You may wish to hide the *4FA Westwood 1* canvas for now. Next, tap the image icon in the *Layers Panel*, open the photo album and add the trees as a layer stack, and then merge them. If needed, drag the merged tree layer above the building layer to move the trees to the front.

Unhide the *4FA Westwood 1* canvas, then tap the *4FA Westwood 1* layer in the Layers Panel. Use the *Opacity tool* to turn the opacity of the layer down to 30% (see Figure 7-41). Select the *4FB Westwood 1* canvas and tap the merged tree layer to select it, then use the skills you developed earlier in this lesson to resize and reposition the layer until it matches the size and position of the original. Refer back to Figure 7-37 if necessary. Remember to use the *Add to Selection* and *Subtract from Selection tools* as needed.

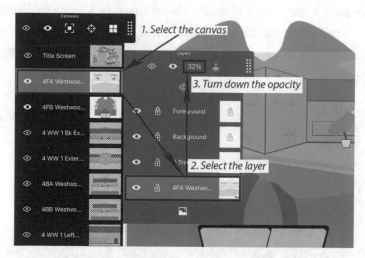

Figure 7-41. *Adjusting the opacity to see through a canvas*

Once you have completed the resizing and repositioning, adjust the opacity on the *4FA Westwood 1* canvas back to full and hide each canvas as you finish. We will repeat the process for the back of the building later in the chapter.

Lesson 7: Canvas Panel Tools Review (3rd Rabbit Trail)

By now, you have probably noticed that Figures 7-39 and 7-40 have areas where the opacity on some of the canvases is not 100% while the *5L Assembled F Canvas* is fully opaque and easily seen. This is an additional feature provided by the *Mental Canvas* team. While the *Canvas Panel* tools were discussed in an earlier chapter, I set aside this feature to discuss here. Therefore, a review of the *Canvas Panel* tools, located at the top of the *Canvas Panel*, is in order. Please refer to Figures 7-42 through 7-47 for this next section.

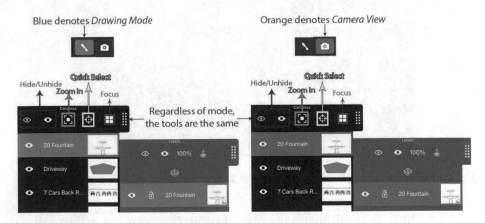

Figure 7-42. *The Canvas Panel tools*

Figure 7-43. *Hide/unhide*

Located to the left of each canvas' name, tapping on these icons hides or unhides canvases. You can hide one canvas or many.

Figure 7-44. *Zoom In*

Located at the top of the *Canvas Panel* in the center under the word *Canvases*, tapping this tool quickly zooms in for a closer view on whichever canvas you are working.

Figure 7-45. *Find a canvas*

Located at the top of the Canvas Panel to the right of the *Zoom In* tool icon, tapping this icon, "when you have a lot of canvases in your scene, this is an easy way to quickly find the one you want. Tap the icon and then drag your pen over the screen until the canvas you want to pick is highlighted. When you release the pen, you'll have selected the canvas (should be highlighted in the canvas panel)." [12]

Figure 7-46. *Focus*

Located at the top of the Canvas Panel at the far right, "this is a handy way to focus on the canvas you're working on. This will reduce the opacity of all other canvases in your scene to make them appear faded, so that it's

---

[12] R. Resnic (Mental Canvas, Personal Communication, March 9, 2022)

easier to see the content on the canvas you're working on (without needing to actually hide the other canvases)."[13] This, of course, is the feature that began this rabbit trail.

To use the *Focus* tool, select the canvas you want to bring into focus, then tap the tool icon. Tap it again to remove focus (see Figure 7-47).

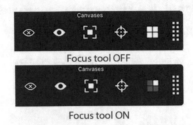

Figure 7-47. *Focus tool OFF/ON states*

(Personally, I prefer hiding the other canvases completely, but I *am* easily distracted by shiny objects.)

Remember the function of each of these tools and refer back to this section as needed while you build out your scene. You will find yourself using one or more of them during the process.

Lesson 8: Duplicating Layers

If you look closely at Figures 7-33 and 7-34, you will see a layer that we have not yet merged or projected – the *6 Assembly Point* layer, located on the *Westwood 1* canvas. The figures show a total of four assembly point images, yet we only have one. Thankfully, the *Mental Canvas* team provided another tool among the editing tools that allows us to address this: the *Layer Duplication* tool.

---

[13] Ibid.

To use this tool:

1. Make sure you are working in *Drawing Mode*.

2. Select the *4FAA Westwood 1* canvas.

3. Select, unlock, and unhide the *6 Assembly Point* layer.

4. Tap the *Selection* icon to enter *Editing mode*.

5. Make sure the following are enabled:

   a. *Editing tools*

   b. *Brush tool*

   c. *Add to Selection*

6. Tap the *6 Assembly Point* image.

7. Tap the Copy (Duplicate) icon

8. Tap either

   a. *Move Duplicate* icon to move a copy of the image to a new location, or

   b. *Create Duplicate* icon to create a copy of the image, then

   c. Verify the duplicate is in the *Layers* list

Refer to Figure 7-48 for examples of all four available options: *Move* a duplicate, *Create* a duplicate, *Project* a duplicate to a new canvas, *Project a Hinged* duplicate to a new canvas.

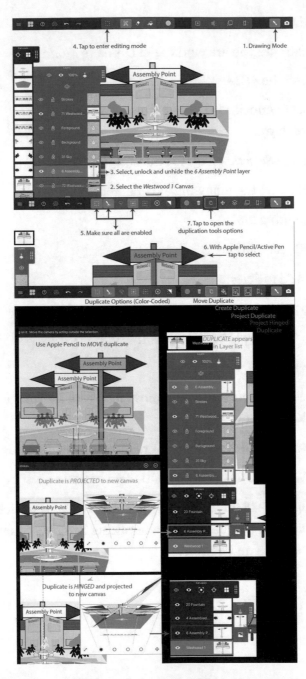

Figure 7-48. *Color-coded explanation of Duplicate options*

Once you have the layer duplicated, follow the steps in *Lesson 6* to merge the two layers, duplicate the merged layer, and rename it *6B Assembly* or some other meaningful name. It will be used with the canvas for the back of the building. Once you have both the front and back merged layers, project them onto new canvases and hide them for now. Your *Canvas Panel* should now look similar to Figure 7-49.

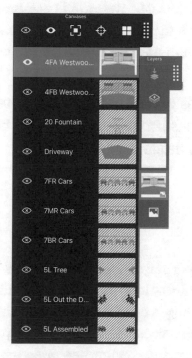

Figure 7-49. *The current state of the Canvas Panel*

At this time, please hide the following canvases:[14]

- Both of the *6 Assembly Point* canvases

- *5L Assembled*

---

[14]**Note:** Some of the file names were changed after the figures were created. The canvas names in the figures may not match the canvas names in the text.

- *5L OTD*

- *Title Screen* (should already be hidden)

- *Driveway*

Finally, unlock, unhide, and select the *4FA Westwood 1* and *4FB Westwood 1* layers on the Westwood 1 canvas and project them as canvases one at a time on top of the *4FAA Westwood 1* canvas. Resize and reposition them to match the size and position of the *4FAA Westwood 1* canvas, then hide the *4FAA Westwood 1* and *4FB Westwood 1* canvases.

Note   The *4FAA Westwood 1* and *Driveway* canvases were used specifically for Lessons *5* through *8* and will not be used again for this project. You may delete them if you prefer.

Summary

In this chapter, we began developing an *Office Fire Safety* presentation using a step-by-step follow-along process. Using skills learned in previous chapters, we began creating a project that allowed us to develop experience and competence importing files onto layers and canvases, projecting layers as canvases, creating new projected canvases, creating hinged canvases, and duplicating layers. In the next chapter, we will use the skills developed thus far to build our *Office Fire Safety* presentation from creating the scene to exporting the final product.

CHAPTER 8

Project 1: Office Fire Safety Part 2

In the last chapter, we began creating our first project. We created our scene, added the project files, and learned how to resize and reposition canvases and organize layers and canvases. We continued developing our skills and experience with the Mental Canvas application, and we chased some rabbits.

In this chapter, we pick up with Lesson 9, Importing Images to Canvas Stacks, and build our project in Lesson 10.

Here are this chapter's objectives.

© Michael Commini 2023
M. Commini, *Mental Canvas for Training and Development*,
https://doi.org/10.1007/978-1-4842-8774-3_8

Objectives

In this chapter readers will:

    a.   Continue to follow step-by-step to create a training intervention using the Mental Canvas application.

    b.   Develop their skills importing images to Canvas Stacks.

    c.   Practice their skills exporting their completed project as a video.

    d.   Practice their skills exporting their completed project for use in the Mental Canvas player.

Lesson 9: Importing Images to Canvas Stacks

Now it is time to import more images. Rather than import them as *Layer Stacks* on the *4FAA Westwood 1* canvas, we will import them as *Canvas Stacks*. Recall this will bring each image onto its own canvas. Refer to Figure 8-1 for this section. The images we will be importing are as follows:

- 4BA Westwood 1

- 4BB Westwood 1

- 4 WW 1 Left Side

- 4 WW 1 Right Side

- 4 WW 1 External

- 4 WW 1 Bk External

- 9 Coffee Hutch

- 10 Rosie 1

- 10 Rosie 2

- 11 Edna the Accountant

- 14 Fire Safety 1 Hall LW

- 14 Fire Safety 1 Hall RW

- 14 FS Exit Wall

- 14 Main Lobby

Should you encounter the five-image limit, you will need to perform this step three times until all of the images have been imported. We will import the rest of the images later in this chapter.

Begin by selecting the *4FA Westwood 1* canvas and open its *Layers Panel*. Tap the *Image icon* to open the *Photo Album* and select the *Project 1 – Fire Safety* album. Select the images and tap *Add*. Refer to Figure 8-1A.

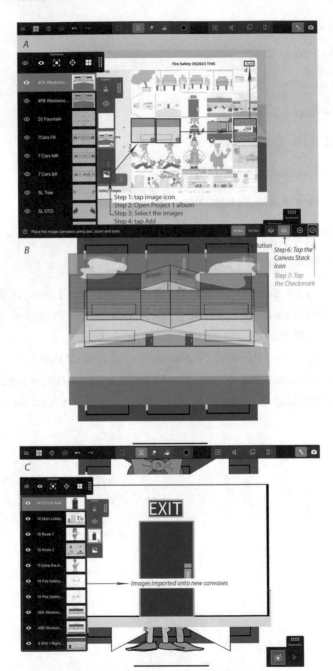

Figure 8-1. *Importing images as Canvas Stacks*

Select the import resolution, then tap the Canvas Stack icon, ,

followed by the check mark icon, , to import each image onto its own
canvas (Figure 8-1B). Finally, confirm all images have been imported onto
their own canvases in the *Canvas Panel* (Figure 8-1C). Hide all but the
Westwood 1 canvas and delete all bookmarks except the title screen and
Westwood 1 bookmarks.

Lesson 10: Building the Presentation

Note   I recommend you frequently save your work during this lesson.

Now that we have completed the practice lessons, this lesson will allow
you to apply everything you have learned. We will start fresh with a blank
scene and use the image files in the *Project 1 – Office Fire Safety* (not to be
confused with the *Project 1 – Fire Safety* album) and *FEMA Images* albums.
Table 8-1 provides a list of the image files used in this lesson.

Table 8-1. *Image files used in this lesson*

Project 1 – Office Fire Safety Images

Assembly Point L1	Assembly Point L2	Assembly Point R1
Assembly Point R1	Cars BR	Cars FR
Cars MR	Cloud Lft Side	Cloud Rt Side
Coffee Hutch	DesignatedSmokingArea	Edna the Accountant
Fire Truck	Fire Warden Fred	Fireperson April
FireSafetyCredits	FireSafetyTitle	Fountain
Fred on Fire 1	Fred on Fire 2	Fred on Fire 3

(continued)

Table 8-1. (*continued*)

Project 1 – Office Fire Safety Images

Fred on Fire 4	Fred Walking 1	Fred Walking 2
Fred Walking 3	Fred Walking 4	Ground
Main Lobby	PlanterTree	Priscilla A
Priscilla B	Priscilla C	Priscilla D
Rosie 1	Rosie 2A	Rosie 2B
Rosie 2C	Sky	Stacked Boxes
TitleSlide 1	Training Wall L	Training Wall R
Transition (blank)	TrashcanFire	TrashOverflow1
TrashOverflow2	Tree Left	Tree Right
WW 1 B Door Open	WW 1 Drive	WW 1 Lt DO
WW 1 Rt DO	WW F Door Open	

FEMA Images

FEMA FrExtTyp	UsingFireExtinguishers	FEMA 12 inches
FEMA Workplace Safety 1		FEMA StopDropRoll
FEMA Workplace Safety 2		FEMA No Elevators
FEMA Space Heater Safety		FEMA Escape Plan
FEMA Emergency Exit		FEMA TestAlarms
FEMA SnowIce	FEMA Use Ashtray	FEMA NoSmoke02-1
FEMA NoSmokeSleepy	FEMA NoSmoke02-20	

Table 8-2 is a list of the text image files used in this project.

Table 8-2. *Fire Safety Text files used in this lesson*

Fire Safety Text Files		
Rosie2	Overflowing	Rosie1
PriscillaSlack	FredKitchen2	Fred FS Hall
FredKitchen1	BlockedFireExit	Arrow3
Arrow2	Overloaded	Walk-Through
Posture	Overflowing2	OpenFlame
Let's Explore	HighPower	HeatSource
Fred is on Fire	FireExtinguisher	EveryDay
Complacent	Commonplace	But WHY
Arrow	This is Fred	ClutterFree
2FirepersonAprilA	Accessible&CurrentPNG	DesignatedArea
FireExtinguishers	AssemblyPts	FireDrills
FirepersonApril	Obvious	CoiledWire

Because we are working with 100 or so images, I recommend importing the images into the project as individual canvases. This will make it easier to work in 3D space and allow you to move quickly through the build-out phase of the project.

Referring to Figure 8-2, you can see the first five bookmarks use *TitleSlide1*. Rather than paste a static 2D image of the title screen, which is boring and not very engaging, I used the skills developed in the earlier lessons to make a 3D interactive title screen – one that can be rotated, panned, zoomed in, and zoomed out.

Figure 8-2. *Begin with TitleSlide1*

I began the scene by arranging the canvases in an order that made it easier for me to hide/unhide them as needed. Then, I unhid, resized, and used the *Canvas Projection tool* to reposition the *Overflowing Trash* canvas so the trashcan with the flames stood away from the wall. Doing this gave the impression of depth when the canvas is rotated around the axes.

I did the same thing with the *PlanterTree* and *FireSafety* canvases, using the *Canvas Projection tool* to move each canvas closer to and farther away from the *TitleSlide1* canvas until I achieved a nice depth of field. Once the canvases were arranged as desired, I created the first bookmark (see Figure 8-3).

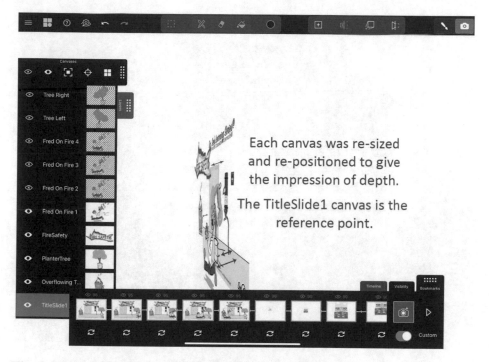

Figure 8-3. *Creating depth with canvas placement*

Next, I unhid the *Fred on Fire 1* canvas and resized and repositioned it so Fred is just entering the scene from the right side of the canvas in front of the planter and tree. Then I created the second bookmark.

The third, fourth, and fifth bookmarks were created by hiding/ unhiding the appropriate *Fred on Fire* canvas. To accurately place the canvases on the same plane as the first *Fred on Fire* canvas, I superimposed each canvas on top of the first canvas, resized it to match the size and position of the Fred character, and then repositioned the canvas so Fred was a little further to the left. I tapped the *New Bookmark* icon each time I achieved the desired placement. When the scene is played in the video or web player, it looks like Fred is running across the main lobby while on fire (see Figure 8-4).

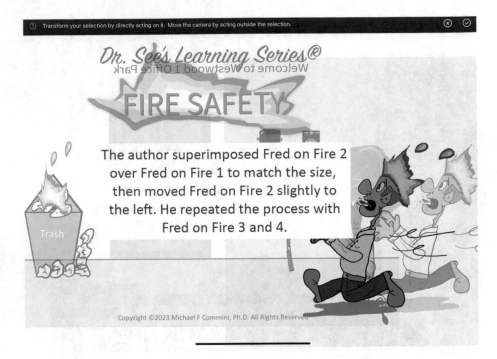

Figure 8-4. *Superimposing the second Fred character to accurately place the canvas*

To enter the lesson proper, I first zoomed out to make it appear the title screen was shrinking; then unhid the WW 1 Drive, WW F Door Open, Cars BR, Cars MR, Cars FR, Fountain, Tree Left, Tree Right, Sky, and Ground canvases; projected, repositioned, and resized them as needed; and superimposed them over the fifth title screen bookmark and created the sixth bookmark (see Figure 8-5).

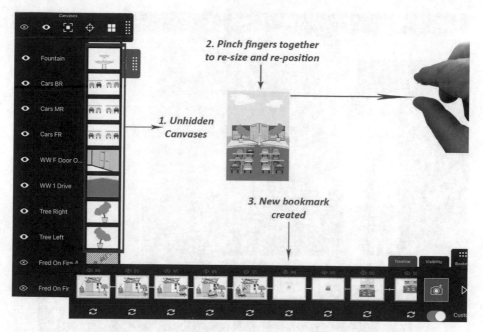

Figure 8-5. *Canvas resizing and repositioning and new bookmark created*

Next, I pinched my fingers apart to zoom in so the building, trees, fountain, drive, and car park were full size and created a bookmark (see Figure 8-6).

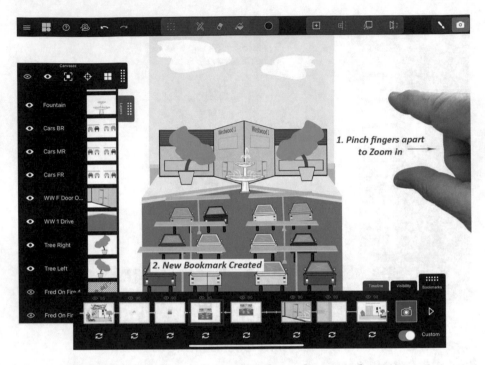

Figure 8-6. *Zooming in and new bookmark created*

After that, I repositioned the visible canvases so the car park was the central point of focus and created the next bookmark (see Figure 8-7).

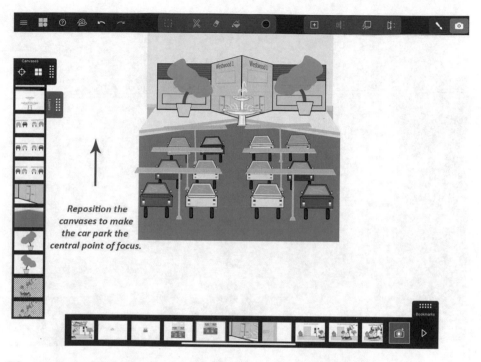

Figure 8-7. Making the car park the central point of focus

This prepared the scene for the next step, which zoomed in over the parked cars, past the fountain and right up to one of the open doors, which is where the next bookmark was created (see Figure 8-8). I next hid all visible canvases and unhid the 14 Main Lobby canvas. I zoomed in very tight and created the next bookmark (see Figure 8-9). Then I hid the 4FB Westwood 1, 20 Fountain, and 7 Cars FR, MR, and BR canvases, and zoomed out so the 14 Main Lobby canvas was in full view and unhid the Fred on Fire canvas.

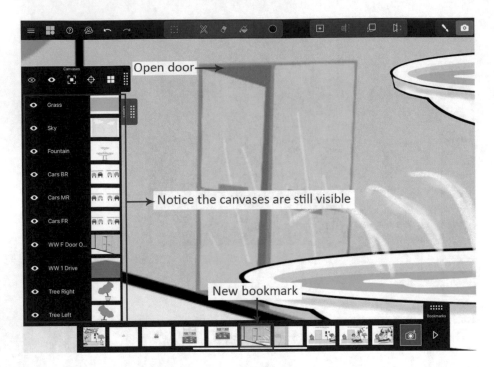

Figure 8-8. *Zooming in to an open door*

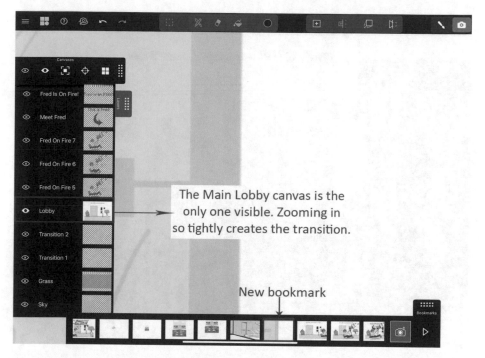

Figure 8-9. *Transitioning to the main lobby*

I positioned the canvas so Fred was just entering the scene from the right – just as we did with the title screen we created earlier. The exception is that with the Main Lobby canvas, the trashcan and the planter are part of the 2D image. Thus, only Fred occupies 3D space. Once Fred was positioned where I wanted him, I created the next bookmark (see Figure 8-10).

Figure 8-10. *Transition to Main Lobby completed*

The next two bookmarks moved Fred to the center of the scene by hiding and unhiding two of the *Fred on Fire* canvases – which canvases you use is up to you. Once Fred was parallel to the door, I unhid the *This is Fred* text image canvas and thus introduced the main character to the learners (see Figure 8-11).

A Quick Review

One item of note: While developing the project for this book, I encountered an issue with the Fred canvases sometimes appearing behind what are essentially the background canvases when they were made visible in the *Canvas Panel* list. This is caused by the Fred canvases projecting behind the other canvases in 3D space during import and can be solved quickly by using the *Parallel Projection* tool. Figures 8-12 through 8-19 provide a visual review for using the tool to change how existing canvases are projected in 3D space.

They also provide a review for resizing and repositioning canvases – in this case, for projecting the Fred character to the front of the other visible canvases as well as resizing and repositioning the Fred character so he appears to be running across the screen.

Figure 8-11. *Introducing the main character*

Figure 8-12 shows one of the Fred on Fire canvases from a previous chapter appearing behind one of the Main Lobby canvases when made visible in the *Canvas Panel* list. The Fred canvas is also quite large.

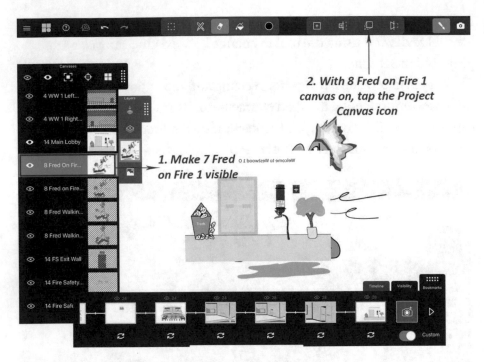

Figure 8-12. *The Fred Canvas made visible*

Using the *Parallel Projection* tool, I used an *Apple Pencil* to pull the Fred canvas to the front (see Figure 8-13).

Figure 8-13. *Moving the Fred canvas to the front*

Once the Fred canvas was in front of the Main Lobby canvas, it needed to be repositioned and resized. Figures 8-14 and 8-15 provide visual instructions for selecting the Fred layer of the canvas and using the *Transform* tool to both resize and reposition Fred.

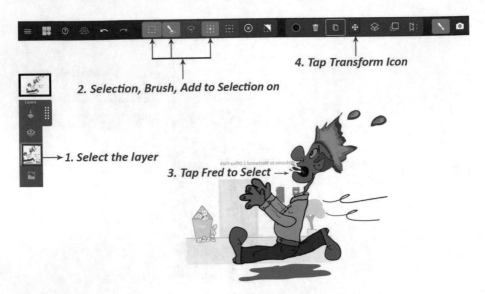

Figure 8-14. *Preparing to resize and move the Fred canvas*

To resize and move Fred, I pinched my fingers together or apart until Fred was the desired size and then used one finger to drag Fred to his new location on the canvas.

Figure 8-15. *Resizing and moving the Fred 1 canvas*

Once the Fred canvas was positioned where I wanted it, I created a bookmark. The only visible canvases were the *Office* canvas and the *Fred on Fire 1* canvas (see Figure 8-16).

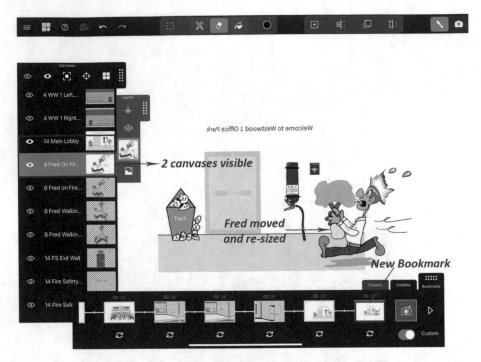

Figure 8-16. *Only two canvases visible for the new bookmark*

You will have noticed there are multiple *Fred on Fire* canvases. They were used to create the animation effect of Fred running across the screen while on fire. After using the same process of bringing the *Fred on Fire 2* canvas to the front and resizing it and repositioning it, I kept both canvases visible while fine-tuning the placement of the *Fred on Fire 2* canvas. I did this for each Fred on Fire canvas used (see Figure 8-17).

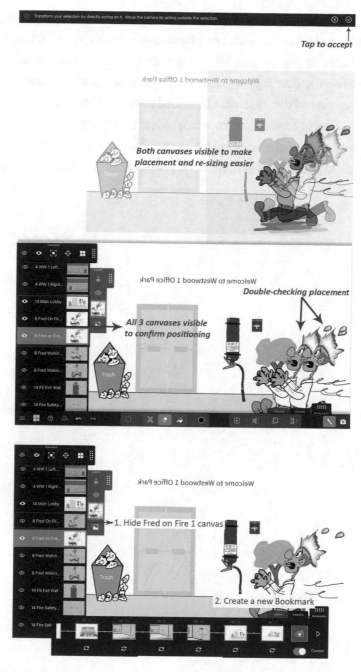

Figure 8-17. *Positioning the 2nd Fred on Fire canvas*

To make the animation effect of Fred running across the screen, it was necessary to make several exact duplicates of both *Fred on Fire* canvases. I used the skills developed in the lessons on importing canvas stacks and resizing and repositioning canvases and layers to match the size and starting positions of the *Fred on Fire 1* and *Fred on Fire 2* canvases and created four sets of exact duplicate canvases. Figures 8-18 and 8-19 show the canvases in the *Canvas Panel* and provide a visual example of the steps I used to create the animation effect of Fred running across the screen.

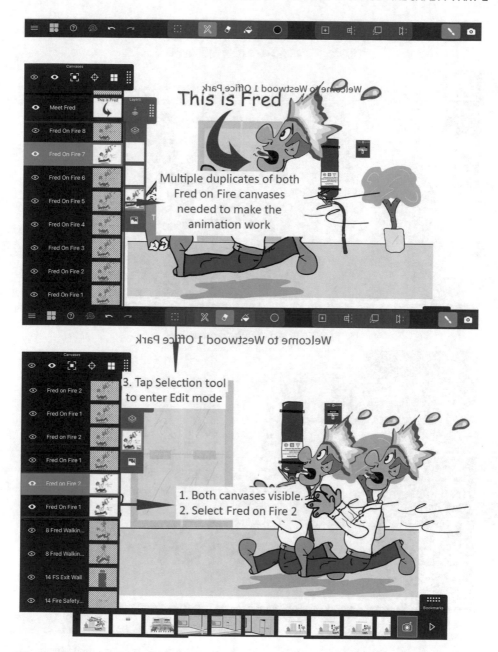

Figure 8-18. *Using multiple canvases to make Fred run – Pt. 1*

Figure 8-19. *Using multiple canvases to make Fred run – Pt. 2*

I then used the second, third, and fourth sets of *Fred on Fire* canvases to duplicate the process and move Fred across the screen.

Adding the Story

By this point in the book, you should have sufficient knowledge, experience, and skills developed with *Mental Canvas* that I no longer need to provide detailed figures explaining each step of the process. From this point forward, I will quickly walk through building the rest of the presentation, including only those images necessary to explain the text. We will now begin adding the story to the presentation.

One drawback with *Mental Canvas* is the lack of a *Text* tool. If your handwriting is as bad as mine, this means you will want to create your text outside of *Mental Canvas* and import it. Of course, there is always the option of writing directly on the canvas. Figure 8-20 provides a comparison between creating your text outside *Mental Canvas* and importing it into the application vs. writing directly on the canvas.

Figure 8-20. *Importing text vs. writing on the canvas*

To write the story text for this presentation, I used Adobe® Photoshop®,[1] but you can use whichever graphics editor you like. Save the text images as transparent PNG files and import them as canvas stacks. Hide them until you are ready for them to appear.

Before moving forward, I recommend you create multiple sets of the *Fred Walking 1* and *Fred Walking 2* canvases (I used 13). Just as we used the *Fred on Fire* canvases to animate Fred's run through the office, we will use the same *Stop Motion Animation* technique to move Fred through the office on his journey of discovery.

Import the Text Image Files

If you have not already done so, it is time to import the text image files. Navigate to the file location where you saved the zip file and open the *Text Images* folder. Select the text image files and import them into your iPad's photo album. You can use the album you are already using for the project images or you can create a new album specifically for the text images. Once you have them imported to your photo album, import them into *Mental Canvas* as *Canvas Stacks* and hide them until ready for use. Your *Canvas Panel* should look similar to Figure 8-21.

---

[1] Adobe and Photoshop are registered trademarks of Adobe Inc.

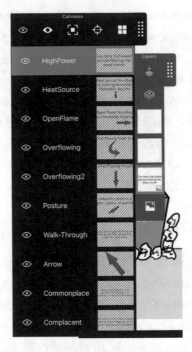

Figure 8-21. *Canvas Panel after importing text images*

Refreshing the Bookmarks

You may recall covering bookmarks in Chapter 6. One of the features we touched on briefly was the *Refresh* button, which is only active when *Custom Visibility* is enabled. As you create or import canvases into your project, you may find them appearing on top of or behind the canvas visible in the bookmark. This is where the *Refresh* button comes in. See Figure 8-22 for a visual example. In fact, you will use the *Refresh* button every time you make a change to an already bookmarked canvas.

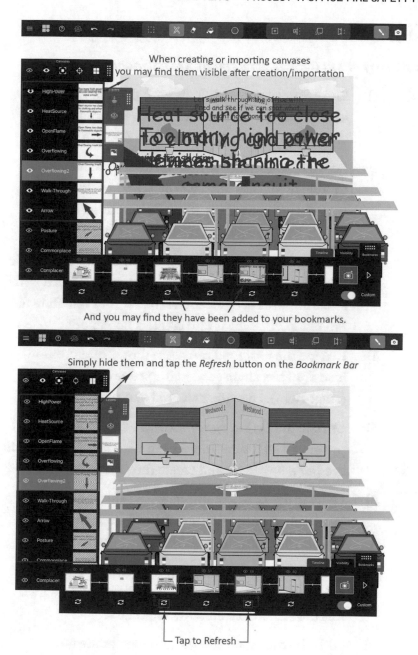

Figure 8-22. *Refreshing the bookmarks*

Building the Presentation (Continued)

Do not worry about timings at this point. We will adjust them later.

1) Picking up where we left off, with the *Main Lobby*, one of the *Fred on Fire*, and the *This is Fred* canvases visible, create a bookmark, if you have not done so already.

2) Leaving Fred in the current position on screen, unhide the *Fred is on Fire* canvas and position it so it superimposes over the *This is Fred* canvas. Hide the *This is Fred* canvas and create a bookmark.

3) Leaving Fred in the current position on screen, unhide the *But why is Fred on fire?* canvas and position it so it superimposes over the *Fred is on Fire* canvas. Hide the *Fred is on Fire* canvas and create a bookmark.

4) Unhide the next Fred canvas in the set and position it so Fred has almost exited the scene on the left (stage right). Hide the first Fred canvas.

5) Unhide the *Let's explore and find out* canvas and position it so it superimposes the *But why* canvas. Hide the *But why* canvas and create the next bookmark.

6) Leaving the Let's Explore canvas visible, hide the Fred canvas and create a new bookmark. This begins your transition to Fred's office walk-through.

7) Hide all visible canvases and unhide one of the two transition canvases. I used Transition 2. Make sure it fills the screen and create a bookmark.

8) Hide the transition canvas, and then at the far right of the screen, make one of the Fred Walking 1 canvases visible.

9)   Above Fred and somewhat centered on the canvas,
      import the text image "Everyday in the office..." onto
      a layer of the Fred Walking canvas. Bookmark it.

10)   Make one of the Fred Walking 2 canvases visible and
      reposition it so it appears Fred has "walked" forward
      a bit. Hide the Fred Walking 1 canvas. This will hide
      Fred and the Everyday in the office text.

11)   Import the "Being a good manager, Fred..." text
      image file onto a layer of the Fred Walking 2 canvas.
      Bookmark this.

12)   Using another Fred Walking 1 canvas, move Fred
      forward again. Hide the Fred Walking 2 canvas from
      the previous step.

13)   Import the text image file that begins "So much so
      that Fred..." onto one of this canvas' layers. Position
      it so it is centered above the door and bookmark it.

14)   Hide the "So much so..." canvas and unhide
      the "Let's walk through..." canvas and the next
      Fred Walking 2 canvas in the set. Bookmark it. I
      positioned this Fred canvas so Fred was just about
      to walk off stage right (to your left as you face your
      iPad's screen). Figure 8-23 is a visual walk-through
      of these steps, and Figure 8-24 shows the associated
      bookmarks.

Figure 8-23. *Visual walk-through of steps 1–14*

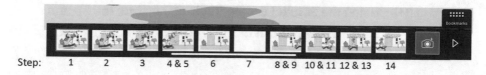

Figure 8-24. Steps 1–14 associated bookmarks

15) Next, hide all canvases *except* the *Main Lobby* canvas. Bookmark it.

16) Zoom in on the Main Lobby canvas, making the fire extinguisher the main point of focus.

17) Make the canvas with "Fire Extinguisher mounted wrong" visible. Align the text so the arrow points to the fire extinguisher. Bookmark it.

18) Hide the text and arrow and zoom out so the entire Main Lobby image is in view. Bookmark it.

19) Zoom in on the Main Lobby canvas, making the overflowing trashcan the point of focus.

20) Unhide one of the Overflowing Trash canvases and resize and reposition as needed so the arrow points to the trashcan and bookmark it.

21) Hide all visible canvases and unhide one of the blank transition canvases. Bookmark it.

22) Next, hide the transition canvas and unhide the Rosie 1, Rosie 2A, Rosie 2B, Rosie 2C, and TrashOverflow2 canvases.

23) Using the Parallel Projection tool, push the Rosie 2A canvas to the back. This is Rosie's cubicle.

24) Using the Parallel Projection tool, position the 2B and 2C canvases in front of the 2A canvas. I placed them midway between 2A and Rosie to give a nice 3D effect.

25) Using the Parallel Projection tool, bring the Rosie canvas to the front, and with all the Rosie canvases visible, create a bookmark.

26) Next make one of the Fred Walking canvases visible. I used Fred Walking 9. Position Fred so he is just entering Rosie's cubical area from the right (stage left). Then import the "Every morning..." text image file (Rosie1) onto one of that canvas' layers and position it near the top of the 2A canvas. Bookmark it.

27) Now, zoom in on the shelf with the candle. Hide the Fred canvas and unhide the Every morning canvas – that's the canvas with the text that reads "And every morning Fred misses:". Bookmark it.

28) Zoom out a bit, hide the Every morning canvas and unhide the Open flame canvas. Resize and reposition it so the arrow is pointing to the candle with the open flame. Bookmark this.

29) Zoom out and pan to the overflowing trashcan and make one of the overflowing trashcan canvases visible. Resize and reposition the image to point to the trashcan. Bookmark it.

30) Hide the text image and zoom back out to the size of the canvases in step 16. An easy way to ensure you have the exact same size is to select that bookmark, create a duplicate of it by tapping the *Camera* icon, and then drag the duplicate to the right end of the *Bookmarks Panel*.

31) Hide the previously used Fred Walking canvas and unhide the next Fred Walking canvas in the set. Position it so Fred is walking out of the scene stage right (to the left). Bookmark it.

32) Hide the Rosie and text image canvases and make the *Coffee Hutch, Edna the Accountant,* and the next Fred Walking canvases visible. Resize and reposition as needed. Make sure Edna is not blocking any of the equipment or the overloaded outlets.

33) Select the Fred Walking canvas from step 32 and import the FredKitchen1 text onto one of its layers. That is the text that reads "Next, Fred stops by the kitchen for his morning cup o'joe. Still, he misses:". Use the Mental Canvas paintbrush to apply a light coating of white paint behind the text if needed. Bookmark it. Figure 8-25 is a walk-through of steps 15 through 33.

34) Hide the Edna and Fred canvases and zoom in on the appliances.

35) Unhide the *"Too many high power..."* canvas, and resize and reposition it as needed. Because the canvas is transparent, it is difficult to read the text. To solve this, I opened the canvas' *Layers Panel* and placed a layer under the text image. I then chose the *Paint Brush* from the *Mental Canvas Brush tools* and painted a white swatch behind the text file (see Figure 8-26).

36) Select the *Too Many Devices* canvas and import an Arrow text image onto one of the layers. Resize the arrow as needed and then duplicate the layer several times. Position each arrow so it is pointing at one of the appliances. Bookmark it.

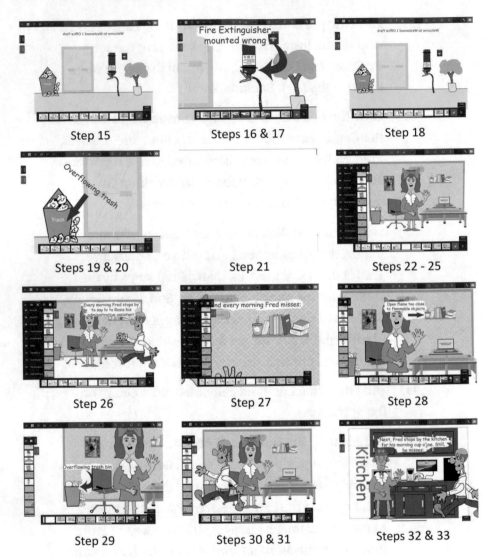

Figure 8-25. *Visual walk-through of steps 15 through 33*

Figure 8-26. Combining imported images and Mental Canvas tools

37) Hide the *Too Many Devices* canvas and unhide the *Overloaded extension strip* canvas. Reposition and resize the canvas and then import an Arrow text image onto one of the layers. I included another white paint swatch under the text image and angled the arrow under it. Bookmark it.

38) Unhide the Edna canvas and pan and zoom in to Edna. She can clearly be seen smoking a cigar.

39) Unhide the Undesignated Smoking canvas, resize and reposition as needed, and then create a bookmark.

40) Unhide the next Fred Walking canvas so it appears Fred is walking out of the scene stage right. Bookmark it.

41) Hide all visible canvases and then unhide one of the blank transition canvases. Bookmark it.

42) Hide the transition canvas and unhide the *Priscilla A, B, and C, next Fred Walking,* and *PriscillaSlack* canvases.

43) Using the *Parallel Projection* tool, push the Priscilla B canvas to the back. This is Priscilla's cubicle.

44) Using the *Parallel Projection* tool, project the Priscilla A and Priscilla C canvases so they are sitting in front of the Priscilla B canvas. Priscilla should be positioned so her feet are propped up on the desk.

45) Unhide the *PriscillaSlack* canvas. That is the one that begins "Then he passes by Priscilla's cubicle...." Because the text was hard to read, I added a layer to this canvas and painted a gray swatch under the text. Then I bookmarked the canvas.

46) Next, zoom in on Priscilla sitting on her ball and leaning against the cubicle side panel. Unhide the Bad Posture canvas – this is the one with the Posture text image file. Be sure the arrow is pointing toward Priscilla. Bookmark it.

47) Hide the Bad Posture canvas and pan and zoom to the desktop with the heater sitting close to Priscilla's shoes. Unhide the Heat Source canvas and create a bookmark.

48) Pan slightly to the right and unhide the Coiled Wire canvas. Resize and reposition as needed so the arrow points toward the heater wire. Bookmark it.

49) Zoom back out so the Priscilla A, B, and C and Fred Walking 13 canvases are in full view. All other canvases should be hidden.

50) Position Fred so he is walking off stage right. Create a bookmark.

51) Hide all canvases and unhide the *Exit Wall* canvas. Bookmark it.

52) Next, create new hinged canvases at 60-degree angles to the left and right side of the *Exit Wall* canvas. These will become your training wall canvases, *Training Wall L* and *Training Wall R*.

53) Create a new hinged canvas at an approximately 60-degree angle from the bottom of the Exit Wall canvas. This will be your Floor canvas (see Figure 8-27).

54) Import the FEMA images onto layers of your training wall canvases. Which images you place on which wall is up to you. Resize and reposition the images as needed. (**Note:** Each canvas will be front and center as you work on it. This means you are importing the images directly in front of the camera. When you return to the Exit Wall canvas, your images will have the correct perspective view as the walls rotate into position. See Figure 8-28.)

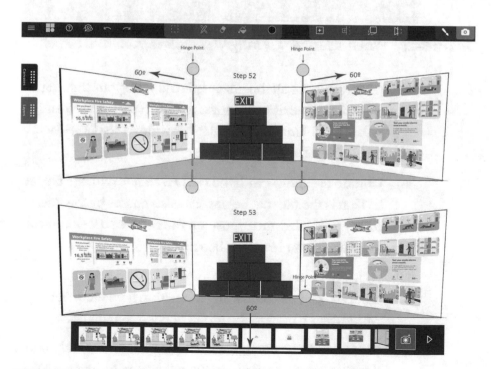

Figure 8-27. *The Hinge Points for the hinged canvases*

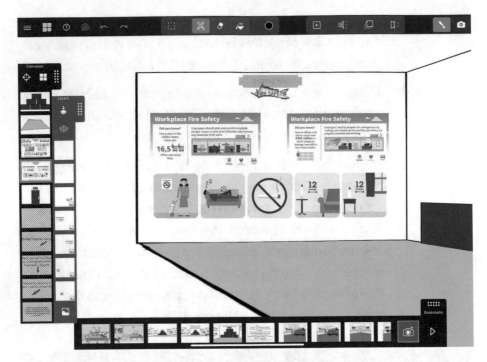

Figure 8-28. *When selected, the hinged canvas is front and center*

55) Once you have all the images placed onto your training walls, tap the Exit Wall canvas to return to that view and create a bookmark. Figure 8-29 provides a visual walk-through of steps 34 through 55.

56) Unhide the canvas with the *Fred FS Hall* text image file on it. That is the file that begins "He also passes by the Fire Safety…." Resize and reposition the canvas so it sits above the Exit sign and create a bookmark.

57) Hide the Fred FS Hall canvas and unhide the "Fire exit is blocked" canvas. Resize and reposition if needed. Add a white swatch behind the text, if needed. Bookmark it.

58) Hide all visible canvases and make a new canvas and import the Title Screen onto a layer. Turn the opacity down to 30%.

59) Import the *Obvious* text image onto a layer above the
title screen. The obvious image is the one with the text
that begins "By now it's obvious...." Resize and reposition
it as necessary and make sure its opacity is set to 100%.
Bookmark it.

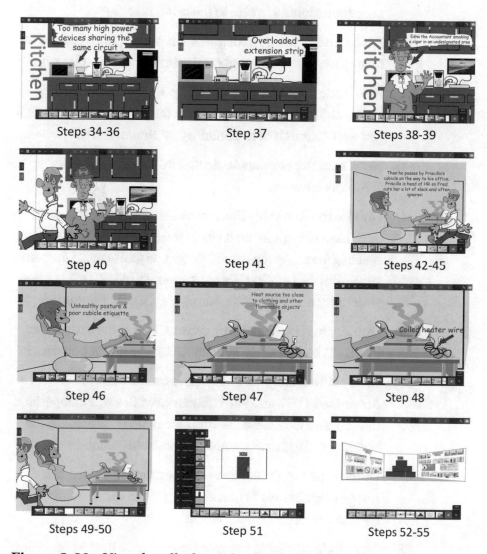

Figure 8-29. *Visual walk-through of steps 34 through 55*

60) It is now time to introduce Fireperson April from the local fire department. Hide all canvases currently visible, then unhide the *Driveway, Building Front, Fire Truck, Fireperson April, Ground, Sky*, and *Meet April canvases.* Resize and reposition as needed so Fireperson April and the Fire Truck are proportionate in size to the other canvases.

61) Resize and reposition the Meet Fireperson April canvas so it sits just over the top part of the building. Bookmark this.

62) Next, hide the Meet Fireperson April canvas and unhide the Walk Through canvas – that is the one that begins "After her walk-through of the building…." Bookmark it.

63) Now, hide the Fireperson April, Fire Truck, and Walk-through canvases.

64) Unhide the Assembly Point canvases. Resize and reposition each assembly point so it sits to the left and right side of the building front. Use the Parallel Projection tool to move the points away from the building. This will present a nice 3D effect when your users pan and rotate during playback in the web player.

65) Unhide the The First Thing canvas. This is the canvas that begins "The first thing she did…." Create a new bookmark.

66) Next, hide the The First Thing canvas and unhide the Assembled, OTD, and Fire Drill canvases. Resize and reposition the canvases as necessary so the office workers are exiting the building and gathering around the assembly points.

67) Unhide the FireDrills canvas. This should have the text image file that says "Then she taught the team to hold regular fire drills." Bookmark it.

68) Next, hide all visible canvases and unhide the Using FrExt canvas. This should have the FEMA image called UsingFireExtinguishers on one of its layers. Create a bookmark.

69) Unhide the Proper Use canvas. This has the text that begins "She made sure they...." Bookmark it.

70) Hide all canvases.

71) Unhide the Exit Wall, Training Wall L, Training Wall R, Floor, and Clutter Free canvases. The Clutter Free canvas should have the text that reads "Fireperson April also made sure the team knew to keep the fire exits accessible and free of clutter." Resize and reposition the Clutter Free canvas so it sits center stage. Bookmark this.

72) Hide all visible canvases.

73) Unhide the *Front*, *Left*, *Back*, and *Right* canvases. Using the Hinge tool, place the Front and Left canvases so they sit 90 degrees to each other. Do the same for the Front and Right canvases. And again, for the Left and Back canvases and the Right and Back canvases. This will allow your learners to rotate around the building in 3D space when they view your presentation through the web player.

74) Once you have the four canvases arranged, unhide the *EdnaSmokes* canvas. That is the one with the 11 Edna the Accountant image file on one of its layers. Resize and reposition Edna so she is standing in front of the building to the left of the open door.

75) Unhide the *Designated* canvas. That is the one with the DesignatedSmokingArea image on one of its layers. Resize and reposition the sign so it sits between Edna and the open door. Bookmark this.

76) Unhide the Designated Area canvas. This is the canvas with the text image file on one of its layers that reads "She also had the building manager establish a designated smoking area." Resize and reposition the canvas so it sits above Edna and the sign. Bookmark it. Figure 8-30 provides a visual walk-through of steps 56 through 76.

77) Hide all visible canvases and unhide the *Exit Wall, Training Wall L,* and *Training Wall R* canvases.

78) Bring one of the training walls into front and center and unhide the *Trng Mats Current* canvas. The Trng Mats Current canvas is the one with the Accessible&CurrentPNG text image file on one of its layers. Resize and reposition this canvas so it sits above the training images in the top center of the wall. Create a bookmark.

79) Hide all visible canvases and unhide the Lobby Fixed and Fire Warden Fred canvases. The Lobby Fixed canvas has the End Title 2 image file on one of its layers. Resize and reposition Fred so he is standing away from the wall. I placed him more or less center stage near the front edge of the carpet. **Note:** The End Title 2 image is a static 2D image. Only Fred will give the appearance of standing in 3D space when panning and rotating in the web player. Bookmark this.

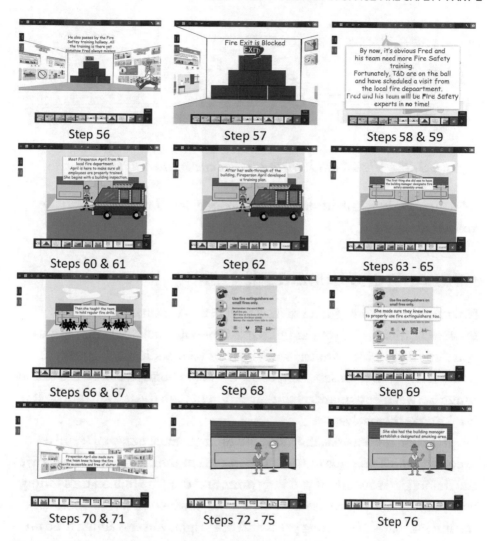

Figure 8-30. *Visual walk-through of steps 56 through 76*

80) Hide all visible canvases and unhide the *End Credits* canvas. This canvas has the FireSafetyCredits image file on one of its layers. Bookmark this. Figure 8-31 is a visual walk-through of steps 78 through 80.

Step 78   Step 79   Step 80

Figure 8-31. *Visual walk-through of steps 78 through 80*

Once you have all the bookmarks created, it is time to establish the animation timings.

Adjusting the Bookmark Timing

Now we come to the second to final part of this lesson: adjusting the *bookmark timings* for your animations. This will entail trial and error as you determine which timings work best for your audience. Figure 8-32 presents a visual representation of the available timings. Notice the timing range between bookmarks is slightly different than those available on the bookmarks themselves.

Between bookmarks, the available timings range between 0 and 8 seconds, with 2 seconds the default setting. For the bookmarks themselves, the default is 0 seconds. If you long press and drag the bookmark's timing icon slightly left, you can select *Pass Through*, which skips the bookmark during playback. If you long press and drag right, you can adjust time on the bookmark between 0 and 8 seconds.

To test your timing settings, press the *Play* button on the far right of the *Bookmarks Panel.* You can play and pause with this button. Just under the *Play* button is the *Looping* button. The default is *Off*. Tapping it turns animation looping on. For those who are not familiar with *Looping*, once your animation reaches the end of play, it will start over again. It will continue to do so until you stop it.

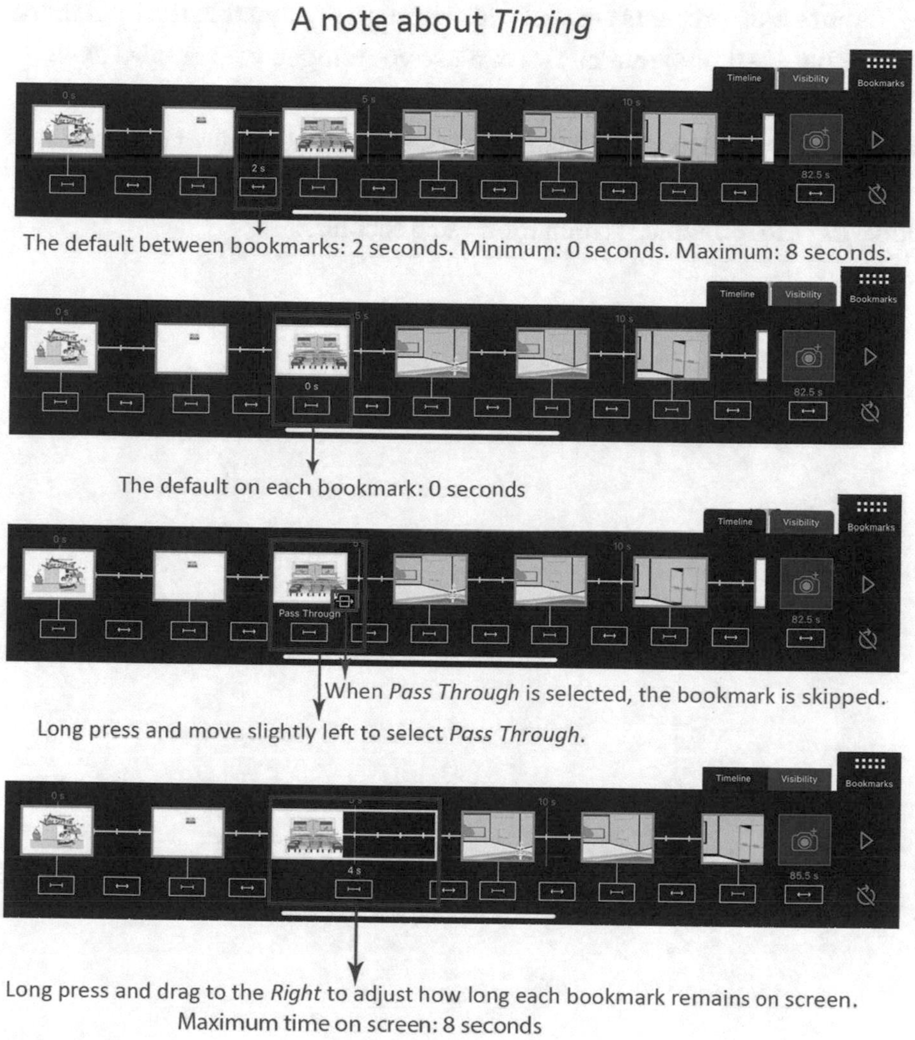
A note about *Timing*
Timeline
Visibility
Bookmarks
2 s
82.5 s
The default between bookmarks: 2 seconds. Minimum: 0 seconds. Maximum: 8 seconds.
0 s
The default on each bookmark: 0 seconds
Pass Through
When *Pass Through* is selected, the bookmark is skipped.
Long press and move slightly left to select *Pass Through*.
4 s
85.5 s
Long press and drag to the *Right* to adjust how long each bookmark remains on screen.
Maximum time on screen: 8 seconds

***Figure 8-32.** The different timings available*

Figure 8-33 presents a visual walk-through of adjusting the bookmark timing between bookmarks. You can use your finger, your *Apple Pencil* (iPadOS® devices), or *active pen* (Windows® devices)[2] to make your timing adjustments. And as seen in Figure 8-32, you can also adjust the timing of each bookmark – a convenient feature to have when you want your bookmark to remain onscreen for up to 8 seconds.

---

[2] iPadOS is a registered trademark of Apple Inc. Windows is a registered trademark of Microsoft Corporation.

Step 1: Tap the *Timeline* tab on the Bookmarks Panel

Step 2: With your finger or *Apple Pencil* (iOS) or
Active Pen (Windows), press and hold the *Timing* icon.

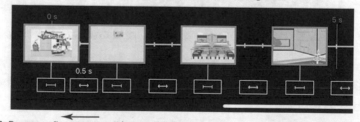

Step 3: Drag your finger or pencil/pen to the left to decrease the time between slides.

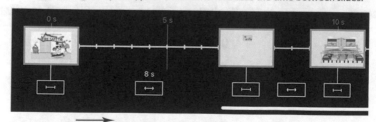

Step 4: Drag your finger or pencil/pen to the right to increase the time between slides.

Figure 8-33. *Visual walk-through of setting the timings*

If you observe your timeline as your animation is playing, you can actually see the progress scrolling along the timeline. Figure 8-34 shows an enlarged view of the timeline with scrolling in progress.

Once you have the timings set, you are then ready to export your video presentation.

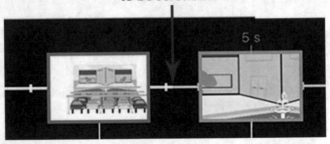

If you look closely at this blown up timeline, you can see the scrolling in progress. To the left of the arrow, the timeline has turned white signifying the part of the timeline that has been scrolled. To the right of the arrow the timeline is still grey, signifying the part yet to be scrolled.

Figure 8-34. *Watching as the animation scrolls across the timeline*

For my final presentation, I had a total of 61 bookmarks. The timings I used are as follows:

Bookmark	Bookmark Timing	Transition Timing
1 (Title Screen)	0.0s	0.5s
2	0.0s	0.5s
3	0.0s	0.5s
4	0.0s	0.5s
5	0.0s	0.5s

(continued)

Bookmark	Bookmark Timing	Transition Timing
6 (1st Transition)	0.0s	0.5s
7	0.0s	0.5s
8	0.0s	1.0s
9	0.0s	2.0s
10 (Door Close-up)	0.0s	0.5s
11	0.0s	1.0s
12	0.0s	1.0s
13	0.0s	1.0s
14	2.0s	1.0s
15	2.0s	1.0s
16	2.0s	1.5s
17	1.0s	2.0s
18	0.0s	2.0s
19 (Blank Transition)	0.0s	2.0s
20	1.5s	2.0s
21	2.0s	2.0s
22	2.5s	2.0s
23	2.0s	2.0s
24	0.0s	2.0s
25 (Fire Ext Mounted)	1.0s	2.0s
26	0.0s	2.0s
27	1.0s	2.0s
28 (Blank Transition)	0.0s	2.0s

(continued)

Bookmark	Bookmark Timing	Transition Timing
29 (1st Rosie)	0.0s	2.0s
30	1.5s	1.0s
31	1.0s	1.0s
32	1.0s	1.0s
33	1.0s	1.0s
34	0.5s	0.5s
35 (1st Edna)	2.5s	1.0s
36	2.5s	1.0s
37	1.5s	1.0s
38	2.5s	0.5s
39	0.5s	0.5s
40 (Blank Transition)	0.0s	0.5s
41 (1st Priscilla)	4.0s	0.5s
42	2.5s	0.5s
43	2.5s	0.5s
44	1.0s	1.0s
45	1.0s	1.0s
46 (1st Trng Wall)	1.0s	0.5s
47	3.5s	0.5s
48	1.5s	0.5s
49 (By now…)	5.5s	0.5s
50 (1st April)	3.5s	0.5s
51	2.5s	0.5s

(continued)

Bookmark	Bookmark Timing	Transition Timing
52	2.5s	0.5s
53	2.0s	0.5s
54 (1st Fire Ext)	2.0s	0.5s
55	2.5s	0.5s
56 (Trng Wall)	3.0s	0.5s
57 (1st Designated)	0.5s	0.5s
58	2.5s	0.5s
59	4.0s	0.5s
60	4.0s	0.5s
61 (Credits)	2.5s	N/A
Total Time:	94.5s	59.5s
	154s/2.566 minutes[3]	

Exporting Your Video Presentation

Exporting your video presentation was covered extensively in Chapter 6. For those who chose to skip directly to this project, the material is presented here again in its entirety. For those who read Chapter 6, feel free to skip to the next project.

---

[3] Be sure to use longer times for those bookmarks that need to be read. These times are for demonstration purposes only.

As seen in Figure 8-35, to export your presentation, you tap the *hamburger menu.* I suggest that you first tap *Save* to save your work and then tap the *Export* submenu to open the *Export Settings* window (see Figure 8-36). Here, you will notice that there are two export options: we can export as *video* for use on YouTube™, Vimeo®, Vevo®, your organization's LMS, or some other form of video delivery,[4] or we can export as a series of *screenshots* for use in a *PowerPoint*® presentation, an *Adobe® PDF* training manual, or some other media format.[5]

---

[4] YouTube is a trademark of Google LLC. Vimeo is a registered trademark of Vimeo.com Inc. Vevo is a registered trademark of Vevo LLC.

[5] PowerPoint is a registered trademark of Microsoft Corporation. Adobe is a registered trademark of Adobe Inc.

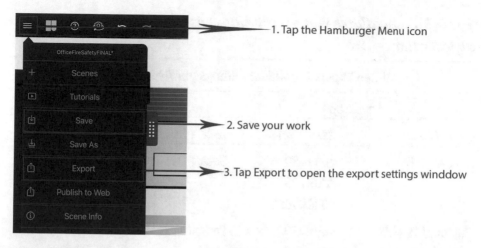

Figure 8-35. *Exporting your presentation*

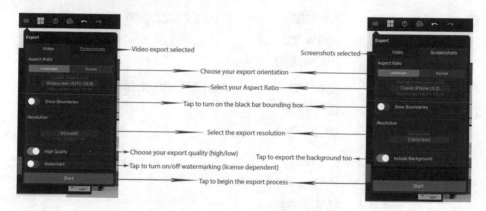

Figure 8-36. *Exporting as video and screenshots comparison*

The settings you select in the *Export Settings* window determine how your presentation appears in whichever export method you choose, video or screenshot, and include the ability to export in *landscape* or *portrait* orientation. As seen in Table 8-3, video *resolution* choices are dependent on the chosen *aspect ratio*.

Table 8-3. *Available video resolutions based on the chosen aspect ratio*

Video Export Resolution Settings per Aspect Ratio			
Landscape		Portrait	
Aspect Ratio	Resolution	Aspect Ratio	Resolution
Square (1:1)	480×480 720×720 1080×1080	Square (1:1)	480×480 720×720 1080×1080
Standard TV (4:3)	640×480 960×720 1440×1080	Portrait TV (3:4)	480×640 720×960 1080×1440
Classic iPhone (3:2)	720×480 1080×720 1620×1080	Classic iPhone (2:3)	480×720 720×1080 1080×1620
Widescreen HDTV (16:9)	853×480 1280×720 1920×1080	Portrait HDTV (9:16)	480×853 720×1280 1080×1920
Ultra-widescreen (21:9)	1120×480 1680×720 2520×1080		

Table 8-4 shows the *resolution* choices available when you export *screenshots*. ***Note***: When saving screenshots, you lose the ability to choose export quality or to watermark but you gain the ability to include or exclude the *Background*.

Table 8-4. *Screenshot resolution settings based on the chosen aspect ratio*

Screenshot Export Resolution Settings per Aspect Ratio			
Landscape		Portrait	
Aspect Ratio	*Resolution*	*Aspect Ratio*	*Resolution*
Square (1:1)	480×480	Square (1:1)	480×480
	720×720		720×720
	1080×1080		1080×1080
	1440×1440		1440×1440
Standard TV (4:3)	640×480	Portrait TV (3:4)	480×640
	960×720		720×960
	1440×1080		1080×1440
	1920×1440		1440×1920
Classic iPhone (3:2)	720×480	Classic iPhone (2:3)	480×720
	1080×720		720×1080
	1620×1080		1080×1620
	2160×1440		1440×2160
Widescreen HDTV (16:9)	853×480	Portrait HDTV (9:16)	480×853
	1280×720		720×1280
	1920×1080		1080×1920
	2560×1440		1440×2560
Ultra-widescreen (21:9)	1120×480		
	1680×720		
	2520×1080		
	3360×1440		

Showing Aspect Ratio Boundaries

You may have noticed the toggle for *Show Boundaries* in the middle of the *Export Settings* window. *Aspect Ratio* dependent, when enabled, the software places a black bounding box around your video/screenshots similar to what you would see on your Smart TV[6] (see Figure 8-37).

---

[6] Smart TV is a registered trademark owned by LG Electronics Inc.

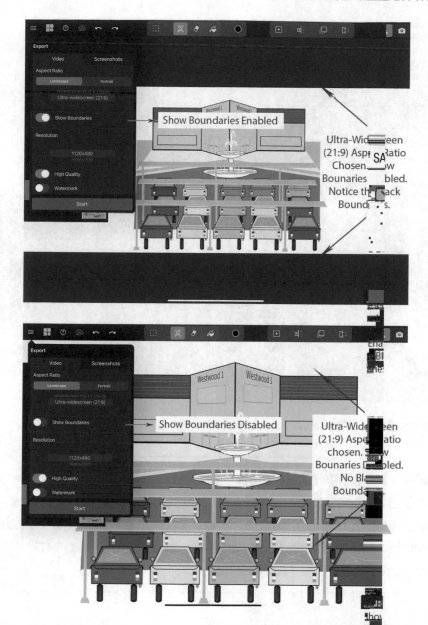

Figure 8-37. *Comparison: Show Boundaries enabled vs. disabled*

The settings I used when I exported my video are presented in Figure 8-38.

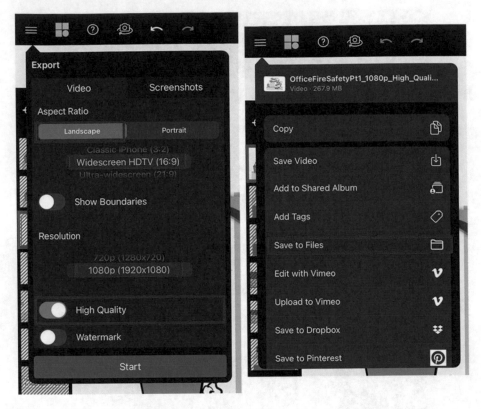

Figure 8-38. *The export settings used by me*

Note There was a several seconds delay between the time I tapped the Start button and the time I was given a choice of where to save the output. During that time, nothing happened on-screen to indicate anything was happening. You can view the uploaded video here: https://youtu.be/loM8wR3pHt4.

Figure 8-39 is a visual example of exporting your presentation as a series of screenshots after tapping the hamburger menu and selecting Export:

a.   Tap the Screenshots tab and select your export settings.

b.   Tap Start. The process can take a while, and there is no indication on-screen that anything is happening.

c.   Choose the location to which to save.

d.   Verify your screenshots have been saved successfully.

Besides the option to export your presentation as either a video or a series of screenshots, you have the option of publishing your presentation to the Web for use in the *Mental Canvas web player*. The next section provides a step-by-step walk-through of the publishing to Web process.

Figure 8-39. *Exporting screenshots to a file location on iPad Pro*

Exporting Your Web Player Presentation

Publishing your presentation to the Web was covered extensively in Chapter 6. Figure 8-40 provides a set of visual instructions for those who chose to skip directly to this project.

Figure 8-40. *Steps to publishing on the Web*

1. Tap the hamburger menu.

2. Tap *Pubish to Web*.

3. Give your presentation a name.

4. Tap *Publish* to begin the publishing process.

5. Once the file has published, you can choose to open it in your browser application or copy the link to share.

6. Tap the *X* to close the window.

You can return to the Publish to Web window at any time to view your presentation in a web browser, copy the link for sharing, or delete the presentation (see Figure 8-41).

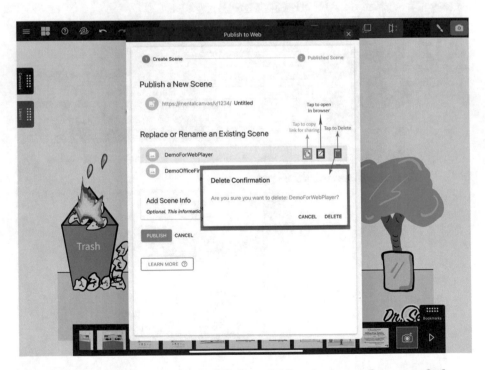

Figure 8-41. *Return to the Publish to Web window when needed*

Summary

This chapter provided a step-by-step walk-through of creating a safety presentation from start to finish. We created a project that allowed us to develop competence using the *Mental Canvas* application with 2D images created outside the application. Using the skills we learned in previous chapters, we gained experience importing files as canvas stacks, creating bookmarks and adjusting animation timings, exporting the presentation as video and screenshots, and publishing the presentation to the Web for use in the *Mental Canvas web player*. In the next chapter, we will create a project directly in the *Mental Canvas* application.

In His Own Words – Abhisek

My name is Abhisek Biswas and I am a storyboard artist, 2D animator, and an indie filmmaker from India. I have been working in the animation film industry for 14 years now. As a filmmaker, it is crucial for me to keep myself updated with the latest tools and technologies in the field. This is why I was quite intrigued when I first heard about Mental Canvas, a software that boasts unique tools capable of creating a 3D space using 2D drawings.

Working with mixed media, such as combining 2D and 3D elements, can be expensive. Additionally, learning a 3D software can be time-consuming due to the technicalities and multitude of tools involved. In such situations, using Mental Canvas is quite convenient for me. The software has a limited but useful set of tools that make it easy to create a 3D space, thereby saving both time and money. This makes it a production-friendly software.

Primarily, I use Mental Canvas to create backgrounds, sets, and animatics for movies in order to achieve a 3D look. I can move my camera smoothly in the particular 3D space that I create and then animate the characters using 2D software to match the background perfectly. This process is not only efficient but also results in better quality outputs.

Lately, I have also been using Mental Canvas to create 3D pop-up comics. This has allowed me to tell stories in a more engaging and visually appealing way, with 3D panels that produce satisfying results.

The possibilities of Mental Canvas are truly endless, and for any fast production studio, this software is a must-have. It enables 2D artists to create an entire 3D-looking world by using their 2D skills, thereby reducing the need for 3D production.

Thank you for your time.

Warm Regards,

Abhisek

CHAPTER 9

Project 2: Office Safety

In the previous chapter, we used 2D images created outside the *Mental Canvas* application and imported them as layers and canvases into our Mental Canvas scene to create an engaging, interactive presentation for use in the Mental Canvas web player and as a stand-alone training video for use in the organization's LMS,[1] YouTube™, Vimeo®, or other video streaming service.[2]

In this chapter, we will create our project directly in the Mental Canvas application with minimal use of external files. Building the project inside the application rather than importing external images has the benefit of allowing you to see your progress immediately as changes are made, while at the same time forcing you to develop your problem-solving skills while you work with the limited tools available in Mental Canvas.

---

[1] LMS = Learning Management System

[2] YouTube is a trademark of Google LLC. Vimeo is a registered trademark of Vimeo. com Inc.

© Michael Commini 2023
M. Commini, *Mental Canvas for Training and Development*,
https://doi.org/10.1007/978-1-4842-8774-3_9

Here are this chapter's objectives.

Objectives

In this chapter readers will:

a. Follow step-by-step to create a training intervention using the *Mental Canvas* application.

b. Develop their skills adding canvases, layers and images.

c. Practice their skills exporting their completed project as a video.

d. Practice their skills exporting their completed project for use in the Mental Canvas player.

Recommendations

For this project, I recommend the following:

- A drawing glove. Drawing gloves can be worn on either hand and prevent the heel of your hand from accidentally drawing on your device when it makes contact.

- A ruler or straight edge. Because Mental Canvas has limited drawing tools, it is difficult to draw lines with precision. A silicone ruler or straight edge allows you to draw anything that requires lines. **Note**: A ruler without ridges along the edge is best if a ruler is chosen.

- Drawing stencils or templates. Again, *Mental Canvas* has limited drawing and editing tools. Hopefully future updates will see better options. For now, we must find other ways to draw. Sketching is fine for storyboarding or demonstrating *Mental Canvas'* capabilities, but if you want a professional looking presentation without having to create your images in external applications and import them into *Mental Canvas*, you need tools that will allow you to draw professional images. Stencils and templates come in various categories including (but not limited to) architecture, electronics, house design, flow charting, drafting, and lettering.

- For iPad Pro users: *Magic Keyboard*. While there will be times when you prefer to hold your iPad or lay it on a flat surface to draw, a Magic Keyboard acts like an easel and allows you to elevate the iPad without having to hold it.

- Music source including noise cancelling headset. Music allows you to tune out the cacophony of sounds in the office and focus on designing your presentation. And who does not have an office gossip you would like to drown? Er, *out*. I meant drown out....

- Coffee. Lots and lots of coffee. ☺

Figure 9-1 shows me using the items I recommend.

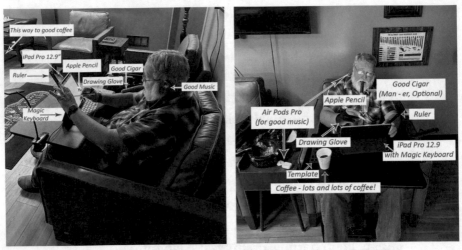

Cigar lounge work area coutersy of Stag Tobacconist, Santa Fe, NM

Figure 9-1. *Me hard at work on Project 2*

Note   iPad Pro users: Your iPad Pro is an expensive tool with a carefully crafted display. Please ***do not*** use anything made of hard plastic or metal against it. To minimize the possibility of scratching your display, use only items made with soft, flexible plastic or silicone.

Lesson 1: Creating the Scene

Since my background is education, and I have been working with adult learners for almost four decades, I believe one way people learn best is through project-based learning interventions. Project-based learning allows for the development and practice of skills and the building of experience. Therefore, this project will be entirely up to you. I will act as your mentor and make suggestions for your design, but ultimately the final product is up to you.

By now, you know that when you open the *Mental Canvas* application on your touch screen device, if you have not yet created any scenes, your app will open to a blank, untitled scene. And if you are starting your project from within another scene, you should save your work before creating your new scene. Whichever is the case in your situation, for this project, create a scene using the *Blank* template. (Notice in Figure 9-2, I used the unique name of *Project 2: Office Safety.* ☺)

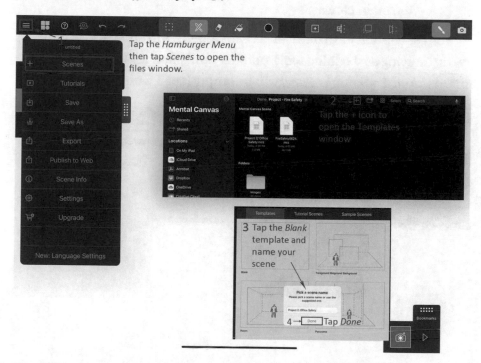

Figure 9-2. *Creating a new scene with the Blank template*

1. Tap the *hamburger menu* in the top left corner.

2. Tap *Scenes*.

   a. *Save* your currently open scene, if applicable.

b.   Choose a location for your scene and tap the
     + sign at the top of your display. (I used the
     Mental Canvas folder on my iPad Pro.)

3.   Once the Templates window opens, tap the *Blank*
     template.

4.   Give your scene a name and tap *Done* to return to
     the main canvas.

Your scene will have one canvas with foreground and background
layers, drawing and editing tools, parallel projection tools, and mode
options. Your *Bookmarks Panel* will be empty (see Figure 9-3).

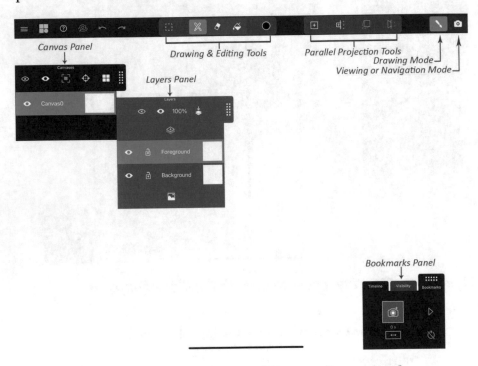

Figure 9-3. *The new scene consists of Canvas, Layers, and
Bookmarks Panels*

Lesson 2: Building the Project

Because we will be working directly on the canvases, it is important to remember that each canvas is transparent, allowing you to see any canvases behind it until paint is applied to whichever section you want to remain opaque. Figure 9-4 shows a before and after example: the top half shows two canvases. Canvas #1 one shows a cartoon profile of a man. Behind that on Canvas #2 is the face of a monkey. Other than coloring for skin, eyes, and hair, the canvases contain no paint. This is proved out in the projection preview window in the top right corner of the figure.

The lower half of the figure demonstrates what happens when a swatch of light blue paint is laid behind the man's profile on Canvas #1. The background layer was used to hold the paint. As can be seen, part of the monkey on Canvas #2 is covered by the paint. The projection preview window shows that though paint has been applied to Canvas #1, Canvas #2 remains unaffected and behind the first canvas.

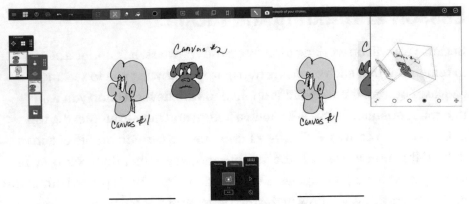

Each canvas is transparent until paint is applied

Figure 9-4. *Applying paint to one canvas does not affect other canvases*

As can be seen in Figure 9-5, it is also important to remember that each canvas is infinite. There are no limits to size. If desired, you could lay out your entire project on one canvas. Of course, that would defeat the benefit of working in *Mental Canvas* – working with 2D images in 3D space!

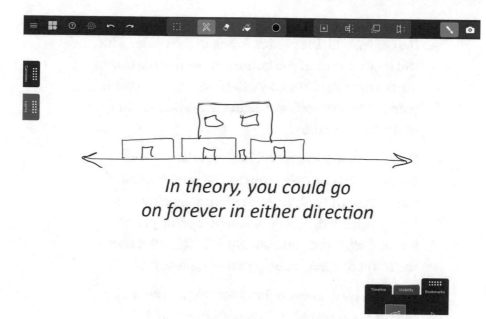

*In theory, you could go
on forever in either direction*

Figure 9-5. *Canvases are infinite; there are no limits*

Now that the preliminaries are out of the way, we can begin building
our project. On your Bookmarks Panel's Visibility tab, enable *Custom*.
By way of review, enabling Custom allows you to hide canvases as you
create bookmarks. The bookmarks you create in this section are rescue
bookmarks. You will create final bookmarks after you have created you
presentation.

1. Begin by naming the first canvas *Frame*. Then create
    a picture frame in the center of the canvas. Fill the
    frame in with whatever color you want but leave
    the center of the frame – where a picture would go –
    without fill.

2. Use a two-finger pinch to zoom in, making the
    frame smaller.

3.   Select white paint and create a larger frame around the canvas with the picture frame in the center. This will be your canvas one boundary. Notice the canvas turns a light shade of gray when working with white paint. This is so you can see the white lines as you create the boundary.

4.   Use the paint bucket to fill the boundary in with white paint. Now every canvas you project behind this canvas will only be seen in those sections you leave unpainted, such as the center of the picture frame. Create your first bookmark. Figure 9-6 shows the result of inking in only part of Canvas #1.

5.   Project a new canvas behind the first canvas and push it backward a bit. This adds depth to the scene. Call this new canvas *Mountain*. **Note**: Hide the Frame canvas to see the Mountain canvas if necessary.

6.   Create a mountain scene on the Mountain canvas. Go as wide as you wish and add as much detail as you wish. Create a bookmark when your mountain scene is finished to your satisfaction.

Notice the screen turns grey when working with white paint

Canvas #1 is opaque except for the inside of the picture frame,
allowing Canvas #2 to be seen in the background.

Figure 9-6. *Before and after: painting only part of Canvas #1*

7. Project a new canvas behind the Mountain canvas and call it *Office Building*. Hide the Mountain canvas. Using a ruler or straight edge, create an office complex. Bookmark it. Figure 9-7 shows my complex to include an observatory.

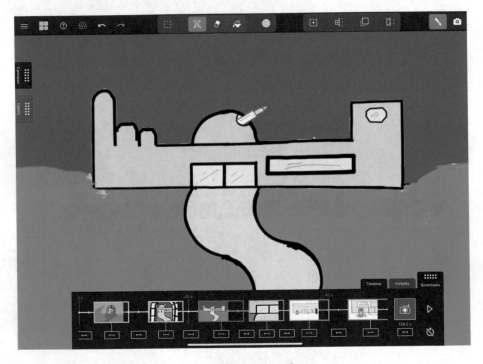

Figure 9-7. *My concept of an office complex*

8. Project a canvas behind your office complex and call it *Inside*. Draw the inside of your office space. Be as detailed as you like. This canvas will be the background for the lobby of your office space.

9. Project a canvas in front of your Inside canvas and draw an overflowing trashcan. For my design, I placed the trashcan to the left of the doors.

10.   Now, project another canvas in front of the Inside
      canvas and draw a fan in front of the lobby doors.
      The cord for the fan should run across your screen
      so someone walking through the doors will have to
      step over it (or trip on it).

11.   Finally, project a canvas in front of the Inside canvas
      and draw a filing cabinet with open drawers. I
      cheated and downloaded an image from Pixabay.
      com. Bookmark it. Figure 9-8 shows my concept.

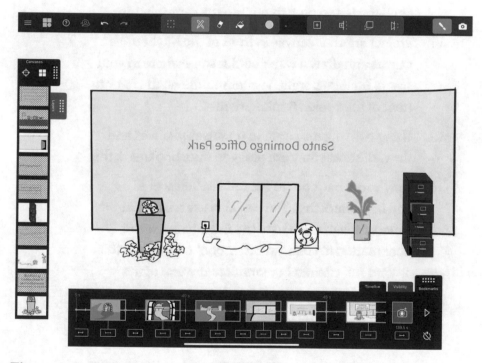

Figure 9-8. *My concept of the office lobby*

12. Project a new hinged canvas at a 90-degree angle to the Inside canvas and call it *Kitchen Wall*. Hide the Inside canvas and draw a kitchen scene on the Kitchen Wall canvas. Add an open door somewhere on the back wall. I placed my door on the right side of the wall.

13. Project a canvas to the front of your Kitchen Wall canvas and draw your kitchen counter. Be sure to include several high-power-consumption appliances and plug them into the same circuit.

14. Project another canvas in front of the Kitchen Wall canvas and draw a water cooler somewhere in your scene. Include a spilled water puddle on the floor in front of the cooler. Bookmark this.

15. Using two fingers, zoom in on the appliances and the wall socket they are plugged into. Bookmark this.

16. Now zoom back out to the full kitchen scene and bookmark this. You can also use a shortcut to accomplish this. Go to the full kitchen scene bookmark and create another bookmark. Drag this second full kitchen bookmark to the end of the bookmarks.

17. Project a canvas to the front of the Kitchen Wall canvas and draw a character slipping on the water. Use the skills developed in previous lessons to resize and reposition the character as needed so they are over the water puddle. Zoom in on the character slipping on the water. Bookmark this. Figure 9-9 shows my concept.

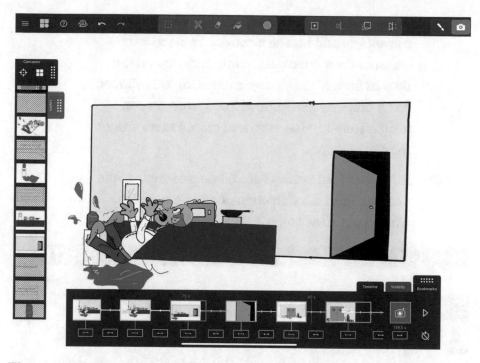

Figure 9-9. *My concept of the kitchen scene with the character*

18. Zoom back out to the full kitchen scene and bookmark this.

19. Now, zoom in on the open door in the back wall and bookmark this. The effect in the final presentation is that you are entering the door to pass through to the next area in your office space.

20. Project a new canvas behind the Kitchen Wall canvas and call it *Storage Room*. Hide the Kitchen Wall canvas. Draw the back wall and a storage cabinet.

21. Project a canvas to the front of your Storage Wall
     canvas and add several hazardous objects to this
     canvas. I drew open paint cans, dirty rags on the
     floor in front of the storage cabinet, an O2 cylinder,
     and a propane gas cylinder. I imported gas can
     images from Pixabay.com and placed them around
     the storage room.

22. Project a hinged canvas at a 60-degree angle to the
     back wall and draw an open door. Bookmark the
     whole scene (see Figure 9-10).

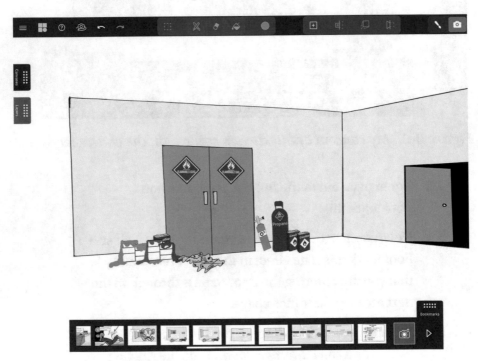

Figure 9-10. *The storage room canvas angled so the hinged canvas
is in view*

23.   Bring the hinged canvas into focus so the open door
      is in front of your camera and zoom in on the open
      door. Create another bookmark.

24.   Project a canvas behind the hinged canvas with the
      open door and hide the Kitchen Wall canvas. Name
      the canvas any name you want. I called my canvas
      Stage. Draw any scene here you wish, being sure to
      include food on the floor and tripping hazards.

25.   Project a canvas in front of the canvas and draw
      a character tripping and slipping. Bookmark this.
      Figure 9-11 shows my concept. Notice Fred is
      slipping on a banana peel after tripping over cables
      and cords strewn across the floor.

Figure 9-11. *My concept for slipping and tripping hazards*

26. Project a canvas behind this canvas and hide the slipping and tripping canvas as well as the character canvas. I called my new canvas Electrical Panel. Draw a wall with an electrical breaker panel. I included an Automatic External Defibrillator on my wall.

27. In front of this canvas, project a new canvas and draw a character receiving an electrical shock. Bookmark the whole scene, then hide the canvas with the character receiving the shock.

28. With the breaker panel canvas still in view, project a canvas to the front and draw a character on the ground unconscious. Bookmark this scene.

29. Next, project a new hinged canvas at a 180-degree angle to the breaker panel canvas and call it Info Board. You will notice the breaker panel canvas is now backward. Following the contours of the breaker panel wall, draw a wall on the Info Board canvas and fill it with the same color you used for the breaker panel wall. This will effectively hide the breaker panel canvas. On the Canvas Panel, hide the breaker panel canvas.

30. Open the Layers Panel for the Info Board canvas and draw information cards. Fill them with any information you want to share with your co-workers. You can also use the information cards provided by me. Include an info card on Workers' Compensation.

31. Draw an AED on one of the layers. Bookmark the finished scene.

32. Zoom in on the Workers' Compensation info card and bookmark it.

33. Zoom back out and create another bookmark.

34. Finally, project a new canvas behind the Info Board canvas and hide the Info Board canvas. Call this new canvas *Credits.* Import the Project Office Credits PNG file, and using the skills you developed in previous lessons, resize and reposition it to center it on the Credits canvas. Alternatively, you can create your own Credits graphic and use that.

Because the *Mental Canvas* app does not have a *Text Tool*, it is necessary to use an external application to create any text bubbles you decide to use – unless your handwriting is nice enough to write directly on your canvases. My handwriting is terrible so I chose to create my text bubbles in Adobe® Fresco® and then import them onto new canvases. You will find my text bubbles in this book's GitHub location. After placing my text bubbles in the appropriate locations, I then went back and adjusted the timings for each bookmark. For my *Project 2*, there were a total of 50 canvases and 47 bookmarks. The following is a list of the timings for each bookmark. Each text bubble canvas is indicated in parentheses, for example, (Office Safety text).

Bookmark	*Bookmark Timing*	*Transition Timing*
1 (Picture Frame)	0.0s	2.0s
2	0.0s	2.0s
3	0.0s	2.0s
4 (Office Safety text)	0.0s	2.0s
5 (Ho-hum text)	2.5s	2.0s
6 (Same tasks text)	2.5s	2.0s

(continued)

Bookmark	Bookmark Timing	Transition Timing
7 (Complacent text)	2.5s	2.0s
8 (Workplace Dangers text)	2.0s	2.0s
9 (Let's Explore text)	2.5s	2.0s
10	0.0s	2.0s
11	0.0s	2.0s
12	0.5s	2.0s
13	0.5s	2.0s
14	0.5s	1.5s
15	1.5s	0.5s
16 (Close-up view of Office Complex canvas)	0.5s	0.5s
17	1.0s	2.0s
18 (Overflowing text)	1.5s	2.0s
19 (Tripping Hazard text)	1.5s	2.0s
20 (Collision Hazard text)	1.5s	2.0s
21	0.0s	2.0s
22 (2nd Tripping Hazard text)	1.5s	2.0s
23 (Kitchen canvas)	0.0s	2.0s
24 (Overloaded text)	2.0s	2.0s
25	0.0s	2.0s
26 (Fred slipping canvas)	0.0s	2.0s
27 (Spilled Water text)	0.0s	2.0s
28	0.5s	2.0s
29 (Close-up of the Open Door canvas)	0.0s	2.0s

(continued)

Bookmark	Bookmark Timing	Transition Timing
30 (Storage Cabinet canvas)	0.0s	2.0s
31 (Improperly Stored text)	1.5s	2.0s
32 (Dirty Rags text)	1.0s	2.0s
33 (Open Paint text)	1.5s	2.0s
34	0.5s	2.0s
35 (Hinged Open Door canvas)	0.5s	2.0s
36 (Close-Up of the Open Door canvas)	0.0s	2.0s
37 (Stage canvas)	1.0s	2.0s
38 (Improperly Routed Cables text)	1.5s	2.0s
39 (Improperly Discarded Food text)	1.5s	2.0s
40 (Electrical Shock Hazard canvas and text)	1.0s	2.0s
41 (Shock Hazards Fatal text)	1.5s	2.0s
42 (Properly Trained text)	1.0s	2.0s
43 (Info Board canvas)	0.5s	2.0s
44 (Proper Training in CPR text)	3.0s	2.0s
45 (Workers' Compensation text)	5.0s	2.0s
46 (Employees Interested text)	5.0s	2.0s
47 (Credits canvas)	0.0s	N/A
Total Time	51.0s	88.5s
	139.5 s/2min 32.5s[3]	

---

[3] Be sure to use longer times for those bookmarks that need to be read. These times are for demonstration purposes only.

Figure 9-12 shows the text bubble canvases' bookmark locations.

Lesson 3: Exporting the Project

Exporting your finalized presentation was covered extensively in Chapter 6 and again as a review in Chapter 7. A quick review is provided here for your convenience. If you have not already done so, save your work. Once your project has been saved:

For Video Export

1. Tap the *hamburger menu.*

2. Tap *Export.*

3. *Choose* your export settings.

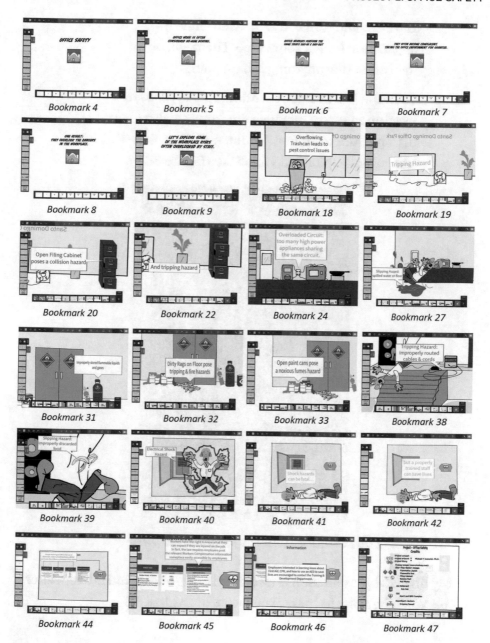

Figure 9-12. *The text bubble canvases' bookmark locations*

4. Tap *Start* and wait a minute or so while the application builds your video. There will be no indication that anything is happening.

5. Once the File Location window opens, *choose* a location to save your video file. You can also choose to Copy, Add to Shared Album, Add Tags, Edit with Vimeo, and Upload to Vimeo (see Figure 9-13).

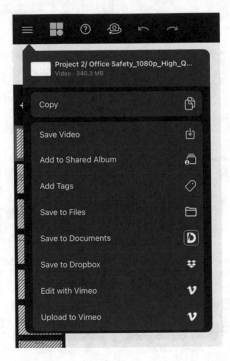

Figure 9-13. *The available choices for video export*

My finalized presentation is available in this book's GitHub repository and on YouTube here: `https://youtu.be/o_sABqgmLaQ`.

For Publishing to the Mental Canvas Web Player

1. Tap the *hamburger menu*.

2. Tap *Publish to Web*.

3. *Title* your presentation.

    a. If this is an existing presentation, choose to replace or rename.

4. *Add* any optional scene information as desired.

5. Tap *Publish* to publish to the Web or *Cancel* to cancel the process.

6. Wait while the application builds your web player version and publishes it to the Web. A progress bar will appear during this process.

7. Once the process has completed, you will be able to open the presentation on the Web or copy the link for sharing (see Figure 9-14).

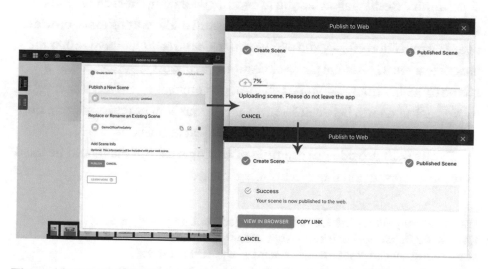

Figure 9-14. *Publishing your presentation to the Web*

My finalized web player presentation is available in this book's GitHub repository and can be viewed online here: `http://mentalcanvas.com/vm/i8zz37x/Project2-OfficeSafety`.

Enhancing Your Exported Video

While your exported video is perfectly acceptable as a stand-alone presentation, there may be times when you want to improve upon it for use in an organization's LMS. For example, the exported video is not *SCORM* compliant, if that is important to you. It is true that SCORM is an old technology, but it is still widely in use today.[4]

And unlike the web player presentation, there is no interactivity between the viewer and the video. The only options presented to the learner are presented in the video playback controls, if it is provided by your system: play, pause/stop, rewind, fast forward. So what can you do to spruce up your video presentation? How can you add interactivity to an otherwise static presentation?

One way is to import your video into software such as *Camtasia®* by TechSmith®.[5] Besides allowing you to capture your computer screen and audio to produce videos, Camtasia includes video and audio editing tools, provides over 100 transition effects, and allows you to create callouts – remember the lack of text tools in Mental Canvas? Camtasia's callouts are another way to create thought bubbles as you scroll through your video – no more having to move back and forth between Mental Canvas and your graphics editor... no more having to project canvases just for your text bubbles.

Figure 9-15 provides an example of adding a callout that could be used to replace a projected thought bubble canvas.

---

[4] ELM Learnng (February 7, 2023). *SCORM vs Tin Can (xAPI) vs AICC: What's the Difference?* Retrieved from `https://elmlearning.com/blog/scorm-vs-tin-can-xapi-vs-aicc-whats-the-difference/`

[5] TechSmith and Camtasia are registered trademarks of TechSmith Corporation.

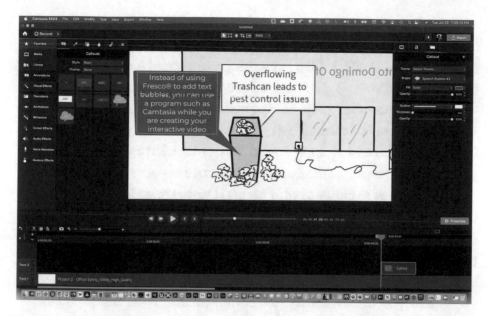

Figure 9-15. *Callouts can be added in video editors such as TechSmith's Camtasia*

Camtasia also allows you to create hotspots. Hotspots are interactive links that "provide a clickable call-to-action in a video."[6] Remember the Workers' Compensation information card on Canvas #45? A hotspot would allow your teammates to go directly to the organization's Workers' Compensation information page on the company website or download a PDF file with all the pertinent information.

Another benefit to enhancing your video with Camtasia: you can add more than one video to your Camtasia project! Imagine adding your Office Fire Safety video to the same project as your Office Safety video, then adding hotspots to allow your learners to move between the two![7]

---

[6] www.techsmith.com/learn/tutorials/camtasia/ add-interactive-hotspots-to-a-video/

[7] While I have used Camtasia since my pre-master's degree days, I am not an affiliate or in any other way associated with TechSmith.

And Camtasia includes some audio editing effects, giving you the ability to add audio to your Mental Canvas presentation. Imagine adding music and sound effects (SFX) or writing a script and having some of your colleagues add voice-over characterizations for the characters you create.

For really complex audio editing needs, *Audacity* is a free, open source audio editor available through its website: `www.audacityteam.org/`. Create, edit, and add multiple sound files and tracks to your Audacity project and then export the finished file for use in your Camtasia project.

Another way to enhance your Mental Canvas presentation video is to use the free software that came with your iPad Pro. And who doesn't like free? I am speaking about *iMovie* of course. iMovie gives you the capability to add special effects, filters, transitions, music, and titles with just a few taps of your finger or Apple Pencil.[8]

Vimeo® provides a robust video editing platform that allows you to create interactive videos. And once you have completed your project, Vimeo will host your presentation too![9]

A simple Google®[10] search for how to create interactive videos will produce over 500,000,000 results, including one for using Artificial Intelligence to help you.

And speaking of Artificial Intelligence...

---

[8] Apple Inc. (2023). *Turn your videos into movie magic.* Retrieved from `www.apple.com/imovie/`

[9] Marano, B. (May 12, 2023). *How to make an interactive video (and why it's worth it for your brand).* Retrieved from `https://vimeo.com/blog/post/how-to-make-interactive-video/`

[10] Google is a registered trademark of Google Inc. Source: `https://trademarks.justia.com/759/78/google-75978469.html`

A Word About Artificial Intelligence

At the time of writing, Artificial Intelligence (AI) is all the rage. Some people love it, some people hate it, and still some people fear it and want to regulate it so we do not have a real-world *Terminator*[11] situation (no lie... there's at least one US Congress person who was recently made a laughingstock because of his proposed bill).

Whatever your feelings about AI, it is here to stay and has quickly become that latest fad tool of choice for every lazy creative in existence. By "lazy," I mean those wanting to take shortcuts rather than take the time to do the work themselves.

Now, do not get me wrong. AI is also a valuable tool for those who do not have the talent to produce content. That is why AI is quickly moving from *Fad Tool* to *Mainstream Tool of Choice*. The benefits of using AI for those who cannot create greatly outweigh the cons presented by lazy creatives. Therefore, I would be remiss if I did not mention AI for use with the Mental Canvas application.

In fact, I used Leonardo.ai to create one of the graphics for the CPR cards used on my Info Board canvas. Did you spot it? Does Figure 9-16 look familiar?

---

[11] *The Terminator* was a 1984 *Orion Pictures Release* movie directed by James Cameron and starred Arnold Schwarzenegger, Linda Hamilton, and Michael Biehn.

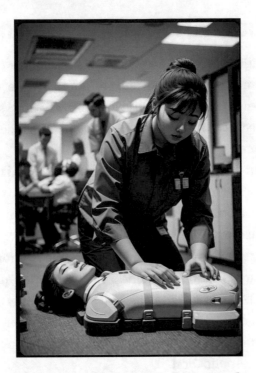

Figure 9-16. *Graphic created by me using Leonardo.ai*

If you look closely at the *Chain of Survival* and *Adult CPR* information cards, you can see the graphic used on the *Perform CPR* and *PUSH* lines of the cards. Because it was original to me using a text prompt created by me, I did not include it on the *Credits* canvas. But could I legally do that?

AI and Copyright

Bear in mind I am not by any means a legal expert. The information I share has been gleaned through hours upon hours of research into AI and US copyright laws. Still, stalwart researcher that I am, there is a slight chance I might be interpreting my findings incorrectly and drawing the wrong conclusions. Consulting a copyright lawyer on your own would be a wise decision. Following is what I have discovered about US copyright and AI.

On September 15, 2022, the US Copyright Office issued a copyright for comic book images created using the Midjourney AI. The images were created as a "direct expression"[12] of the comic book creator's creative thoughts and ideas. In February 2023, however, the US Copyright Office revised the copyright it issued because the artwork generated by the AI was not generated by a human. Talk about not living in the 21st century!

Anyway, the Copyright Office stated that certain parts of the comic book were covered by copyright; they are as follows:

A.   All text original to the author

B.   The arrangement of text and images

According to the US Copyright Office, any artwork generated by a nonhuman is *NOT* copyrightable.[13] The question remains whether or not artwork generated by nonhumans and modified by humans is copyrightable. In all fairness to the US Copyright Office, it has "launched an initiative to examine the copyright law and policy issues raised by artificial intelligence (AI) technology, including the scope of copyright in works generated using AI tools and the use of copyrighted materials in AI training."[14]

One of the reasons for launching the initiative is because many creatives, including Kristina Kashtanova, creator of *Zarya of the Dawn*, the aforementioned comic book, claim that AI is simply a tool used to allow them to create artwork that is a direct expression of their creativity, just as Adobe® Photoshop®, GIMP, Mental Canvas, and Procreate® are tools to allow creative expression. I stand firmly in this camp.

---

[12] As reported by Sunil Ramlochan in the February 22, 2023, article, *No Copyright Protection for AI-Generated Images*. Retrieved from www.promptengineering.org/no-copyright-protection-for-ai-generated-images/

[13] US Copyright Office, *Copyright Registration Guidance: Works Containing Material Generated by Artificial Intelligence*, published in 16190 Federal Register, VOL 88, NO. 51, March 16, 2023. Retrieved from www.copyright.gov/ai/ai_policy_guidance.pdf

[14] www.copyright.gov/ai/

Still, given the US Copyright Office's stance on nonhuman generated artwork, how am I able to claim the artwork generated by me on Leonardo. ai as my original work? The answer lies in the license.

Leonardo.ai states clearly in section 3a of its *Terms of Service* that its subscription users own all content they input for generation and "Leonardo.Ai hereby assigns to you all its right, title and interest in and to Output."[15] Since I am a subscription user, I qualify. Whether or not the US Copyright Office will recognize the assignment is unknown. Perhaps the initiative will answer that question.

Additionally, because the AI-generated artwork was used in the Project 2 presentation and this book, I believe the image falls under the arrangement clause of the US Copyright Office's statement.

AI Prompting

Should you choose to use Leonardo.ai or some other form of text-to-image AI generation to create artwork for your projects, it is important to learn to write good prompts to achieve the results you want. It is beyond the scope of this book to teach AI prompting, but a quick discussion is appropriate.

To achieve a professional result you can use in your Mental Canvas scenes, follow these "rules":

1. The weaker your prompt text, the less likely will be the generated image to match the picture in your mind's eye. The more specific your prompt, the more likely you are to receive the results you want.

---

[15] Leonardo.ai *Terms of Service, Section 3 Content*. Retrieved from `https://leonardo.ai/terms-of-service/`

2. Use the proper AI generator for the results you
    desire. There are many types of AI image generators.
    Some create stunning images that imitate the
    works of the great masters, while others generate
    dream-like, surreal images. Still other generators
    use simple text-to-image prompts that allow users
    to provide simple descriptions from which the AI
    then generates high-quality images. There is even
    an AI generator that allows users to "generate a
    wide variety of images, including realistic faces, 3D
    and anime characters, paintings, backgrounds, and
    digital art of all types."[16]

3. Verify the image generated has not been *stolen*
    from another copyrighted image. It is one thing to
    emulate another artist's style. It is entirely another
    thing for an AI image generator to infringe upon
    another artist's hard work and effort.[17]

Summary

This chapter provided a step-by-step walk-through of creating an office
safety presentation from start to finish. We created a project that allowed
us to develop competence using the *Mental Canvas* application with 2D
images created outside the application. Using the skills we learned in

---

[16] See *The Complete Guide to AI Image Generators (Including the Best Options in 2023)*, The Best AI Image Generators, Section 7, Fotor. Retrieved from https://castos.com/ai-image-generators/

[17] Xiang, C. (2023) *Artists Are Suing Over Stable Diffusion Stealing Their Work For AI Art*. Retrieved from www.vice.com/en/article/dy7b5y/artists-are-suing-over-stable-diffusion-stealing-their-work-for-ai-art

previous chapters, we gained experience using the limited drawing tools available in the *Mental Canvas* application, improved upon our problem-solving skills while utilizing those same drawing tools, imported files onto layers and canvases as needed, created bookmarks and adjusted animation timings, exported the presentation as video for use in the organization's LMS, and published the presentation to the Web for use in the *Mental Canvas web player*.

We discussed various methods of enhancing exported videos using tools such as iMovie, Camtasia, and Audacity. And finally, we briefly explored using AI-generated images and the copyright restrictions that may be encountered by doing so.

The next and final chapter is a wrap-up of the Mental Canvas application and a brief discussion on adult learning and instructional design.

SECTION V

And Finally...

CHAPTER 10

Summary of Our Mental Canvas Journey of Discovery

As we have seen, Mental Canvas lends itself well to the development of interactive presentations for use in training and development. To be sure, Mental Canvas is not a be-all, end-all for training and development professionals, but it is a tool to consider adding to your development toolkit.

During our Mental Canvas learning journey, we explored the licensing options, which include a free license, an Enterprise license, a Professional license, and an Education license. And recently the Mental Canvas team added a one-time Creator license – you pay once to unlock full functionality but are limited to publishing only "1 public interactive web scene."[1]

---

[1] https://mentalcanvas.com/purchase

© Michael Commini 2023
M. Commini, *Mental Canvas for Training and Development*,
https://doi.org/10.1007/978-1-4842-8774-3_10

We also discovered how easy it is to download and install the application to our touch screen devices and to create scenes. And during that first scene creation process, we explored the file management system and learned that we can save our scenes to multiple locations including on our touch screen devices and to external storage locations such as iCloud[2] and Dropbox.[3]

Once the application was installed on our devices and the first scene created, we explored the workspace that included the first canvas, the Canvas Panel, the Layers Panel, the Bookmarks Panel, the Drawing Mode button, and the View/Navigation/Camera Mode button.[4] Which mode is chosen determines whether we have access to the drawing and editing tools or can the camera position of our canvases during the design of the scene.

Also included in the workspace are the drawing tools, which include five different types of brushes and their sizing adjustments, the selection tool, the eraser, and the paint can. A color picker is also available to us. The workspace also includes the editing tools, available through the Selection tool, which we explored in depth when we studied the Layers Panel.

We learned that canvas projection tools are also available to us. They include (a) the new canvas projection tool, for creating and projecting new canvases into our 3D space; (b) the new hinged canvas tool, which allows us to create new canvases and project them at angles to other canvases – convenient for intersecting those other canvases or adding bridges and building sides and other three-dimensional features; (c) the canvas projection tool, for projecting existing canvases in 3D space; and (d) the hinged canvas projection tool, for hinging parts of an existing canvas.

---

[2] iCloud is a registered trademark of Apple Inc.

[3] Dropbox is a registered trademark of Dropbox, Inc.

[4] The Mental Canvas team used different terms to describe the same mode.

Also part of our learning journey was the discovery that each canvas is transparent until fill is added. This feature allowed us to see other canvases and create effects such as fly-throughs from one canvas to another. We also learned that canvases are infinite in any direction in 3D space. This means we can draw our content as far in any direction we want, all on one canvas, though that defeats the main purpose of the Mental Canvas app – placing 2D images, sketches, and strokes into 3D space.

Exploring the Canvas Panel led to the discovery that the Canvas Panel can hold as many canvases as we wish to use – limited only by the storage capabilities of our touch screen devices. We also discovered that the position of a canvas on the Canvas Panel has no effect on the visibility of that canvas in relation to the other canvases. A further examination of the Canvas Panel allowed us to learn that canvases can be hidden and unhidden.

We also explored the Layers Panel, which, we learned, holds the layers for each canvas. Each canvas has, by default, two layers: a foreground layer and a background layer. As in other graphics applications such as Adobe® Photoshop®,[5] layer hierarchy makes a difference, that is, a layer on top of another layer is visible where the bottom layer is not. Conditions apply that allow an exception to this rule and can make for some interesting effects. One such condition is turning down the opacity of the top layer, which allows the layer under it to bleed through.

We can also import images created in external applications into our Mental Canvas scene. Single images are imported onto a layer on the canvas upon which we are working. When importing multiple images simultaneously, we are given the option to import them as separate layers on the same canvas or project them as individual canvases placed on the Canvas Panel.

---

[5] Adobe and Photoshop are registered trademarks of Adobe Inc.

Using the editing tools available through the Selection tool, we learned how to resize and reposition canvases and layers. We also learned how to duplicate layers on the same canvas as well as duplicate layers and project the duplicate layers as new canvases placed in the Canvas Panel.

We also explored the Bookmarks Panel, which allowed us to create rescue bookmarks for use to return to a specific location in the event of making a mistake or encountering a system failure such as loss of power. We also examined the Timeline and Visibility tabs on the Bookmarks Panel. The Timeline tab allows us to adjust how long each canvas remains visible during playback as well as the length of the transitions between one canvas and the next.

The Visibility tab allows us to determine which canvases will appear in the Bookmarks Panel and in the final playback. By enabling the Custom function, we can hide and unhide canvases as we move through our scene. This allows for some pretty nifty effects during playback.

To develop our skills and experience with the Mental Canvas application, we designed two projects. One project used images created in an external application, in this case, Adobe® Fresco®,[6] and the second project we designed in the Mental Canvas application itself using externally created images sparingly.

Both projects were exported as videos and stand-alone, interactive presentations for use in the Mental Canvas web player.

Of course, before exporting our scenes, we had to first examine the available export options, which included the type of export - video or screenshots, the aspect ratios, and the resolution at which our exported scenes were produced.

---

[6] Adobe and Fresco are registered trademarks of Adobe Inc.

We also learned the process for Publish(ing) to Web, which included naming our presentations and choosing whether the presentation was a new presentation or a replacement for an existing presentation. We also briefly explored the optional settings. We briefly discussed copyrighting our presentations.

Also discussed during our journey of exploration was copyright ownership as it applied to our design process and the final product. We learned that all original content – content developed by us – is immediately copyrighted in most jurisdictions, the United States included.

We briefly touched on the use of Artificial Intelligence (AI) to create content for use in our scenes and discussed the current stance held by the US Copyright Office with regard to copyright ownership for content created by nonhumans, that is, AI bots.

And finally, we discussed methods for enhancing our exported videos using tools such as

    a. TechSmith's Camtasia[7]

        1. Adding hotspots for interactivity

        2. Adding callouts

        3. Video editing

        4. Audio editing

        5. Some of the transitions and effects available to us

    b. Apple® iMovie®[8]

    c. Audacity®[9] for audio editing

---

[7] TechSmith and Camtasia are registered trademarks of TechSmith Corporation.

[8] Apple and iMovie are registered trademarks of Apple Inc.

[9] Audacity is a registered trademark of MuseCY SM Ltd.

Besides the positive functions and attributes available to us in the Mental Canvas application, we also discussed two of the drawbacks with the application. They include

1. The lack of sophisticated drawing tools

2. The lack of sophisticated text editing tools

Final Discussion

When it comes down to it, the positives of the Mental Canvas application far outweigh the negatives. Mental Canvas allows us to place our 2D images and sketches into a 3D environment, something few other applications do. And utilizing the interactivity available through the application, our learners no longer have to suffer Death by PowerPoint[10] – something every learner everywhere will thank us for.

From the Author

I thank you for taking time out of your very busy day to share this journey of discovery through the Mental Canvas application. I hope you enjoy using the app to enhance your learners' knowledge and skills building activities and welcome your shared experiences.

---

[10] PowerPoint is a registered trademark of Microsoft Corporation.

Index

A

Adobe®, 93, 165, 277, 304, 335, 347, 355, 356

Adobe Fresco®, 98, 125, 126, 129–133, 138, 147, 193, 205

Adobe Illustrator®, 47, 98

Adobe Photoshop®, 47, 98, 103, 125–129, 147, 193, 205

Adobe Premiere Pro®, 5

Animatics, 4, 316

Animations
   timeline tab, 160–162
   visibility tab, 162–165

Animation timings, 160, 161, 176, 213, 296–303, 315, 350

Animation Timing sliders, 158

Apple®, 357

Apple iPad Pro, 13

Apple Pencil, 5, 13, 27, 59, 72, 124, 196, 201, 219, 227, 266, 298, 344

Artificial intelligence (AI), 345, 357
   and copyright, 346–348
   graphics, 346
   prompting, 348, 349

Aspect ratio boundaries, 169–172, 308–312

Audacity, 344, 350, 357

Automatic External Defibrillator, 334

B

Bird's Eye View Preview Window, 122, 124

Bookmarks, 144, 160, 239, 256, 257
   animations, 156
   bar, 156, 158, 225
   Canvas Projection tool, 155
   creation, 260
   deleting, 159
   Mental Canvas application, 151
   panel, 73, 322, 325, 356
   refreshing, 278–280
   superimposing screen, 258
   text bubble canvases, 338–341
   3D space working, 149–152
   thumbnail windows, 197
   timing icon
      adjustment, 296–303
   TitleSlide1, 255
   visibility tab, 158
   Westwood 1 canvas, 253
   word processing software, 152

Printed in the United States
by Baker & Taylor Publisher Services